Pathways to Publication

Author Publishing Ltd

Acknowledgements

The Literature department of The Arts Council of England for support and encouragement

Many writers and friends for advice and support.

Long suffering Rod Ross.

Our parents and families.

Our students for teaching us to write

and to teach in an accessible way.

Many editors of the past and even more numerous rejecting editors.

All lovers and ex-wives.

Bernie Ross grew up in a family of artists and trained as an art student. She soon found her niche in painting with words and spends every day perfecting her skill. Her accumulated knowledge of teaching adults; hundreds of published articles about nurturing young children's creative play; and writing about all of it as well as writing fiction and drama, is drawn together in Writing Life, the home study course she runs from writinglife.org.uk. Creative Writing the Organic Way forms the course material and - always ready for a new challenge - Bernie shares the same wisdom and philosophy with those who are determined to make the most of author.co.uk

Trevor Lockwood is world-worn. Once a technical author, a policeman, a smallholder, a surveyor, an economist, a teacher and a research fellow at Sussex University. Always an optimistic peasant. A past littered with mistakes now brings him to an exciting present where so many projects beckon for his attention.
The author.co.uk site lies at the core of his being with several new book projects always being planned.
He lives alone by the sea in Suffolk working on the dream that allows writer to reach reader while sipping a glass of wine.

Author Publishing Ltd
61 Gainsborough Road, Felixstowe, Suffolk
IP11 7HS

ISBN 1-898030-17-0

© Bernie Ross and Trevor Lockwood 2002

The moral right of the authors has been asserted.

All rights reserved. No part of this publication may be reproduced, stored in a retrieval system, or transmitted, in any form or by any means without the prior permission in writing of Author Publishing Ltd.

This book is sold subject to the condition that it shall not, by way of trade or otherwise, be lent, resold, hired out or otherwise circulated without the publisher's prior consent in any form other than that supplied by the publisher.

British Library Cataloguing in Publication Data available.

Cover design by Cathi Stevenson from an original painting by Bernie Ross

Produced in Kent
by JRDigital Print Services

Dedicated to our fellow writers

Contents

1	INTRODUCTION
3	**SECTION ONE**
3	YOU WANT TO BE A WRITER?
11	TOOLS OF THE TRADE
19	AUTHOR INTERVIEWS
31	DIARIES AND JOURNALS
39	THERAPY
43	GROUCHING THERAPY
51	**SECTION TWO**
51	LIBERATION!
55	GET A LIFE!
67	CREATIVE FROLICS
71	VIGNETTES
77	WRITE WITH STYLE
87	TRIGGERS
91	TALK AND TELL
103	VISUALISE
127	PLOTS AND PREDICAMENTS
143	THE CREATIVE PROCESS
151	EXPERIMENTAL WRITING
157	FIND YOUR ROSTRUM – GENRES
171	LITERARY CLOUT
181	EMOTIONS
201	ARGUE – AND TRIGGER DEBATE

215	SECTION THREE
215	THE WIDER WORLD
231	YOUR INTERNET
241	COPYRIGHT
245	PERMISSIONS
247	EDITING YOUR BOOK
255	SUBMITTING TO A PUBLISHER
259	LITERARY AGENTS
263	EBOOKS
271	PUBLISHING
279	PRINT ON DEMAND
285	SELLING BOOKS
293	INDEX

Introduction

If you're thinking of writing and publishing a book, or even if you have written one, you may not realise how much work and attention to detail it demands.

Section 1 has points you need to know well enough to incorporate them into your life and into your writing. Equipment does matter, so does professionalism and dedication. Your passion to write must of course be at the coal face even if you have to buy-in a secretarial service; but for most writers this is both impractical and undesirable. Keeping a diary or journal is pretty essential - how else do you learn to put into words these feelings and observations that make for good writing? You need writing experience to be able to express yourself without internal censors, to write with confidence and with a voice that is sure of what it wants to say. This can only grow through practice and through being familiar with your own emotions, your own life experiences as you know them inside and then written on the page.

In Grouching Therapy we acknowledge the need for the novice to experience some freelance work: relationships with editors; the waiting; the rejections; the raised hopes and the disappointments are all part of the learning process through which we have to move and then put behind us. Writers must learn to have empathy with their readers and if you can begin to see the role of an editor from an editor's point of view, then your chances of hitting the right note in your next approach will be all the higher.

Every chapter in Section 2 is relevant for the fiction writer in particular, who must do more than paint pictures in words about the everyday obvious, because detailed observations, style, plot, dialogue and character must all be extra special. You might think you've written a good book and you may indeed have written a good story, but the skill goes well beyond good grammar and a good yarn, and too many nascent writers find it hard to understand this. Writing must be tight, concise and daring if it's to stand out in the ocean of words that arrive on publishers' desks every week. Even if you have an open road to a book-hungry public, people will want to see a good reason for buying your book instead of spending money elsewhere. You can be different enough, you can be a good writer; but practice and experiment and more writing practice will ensure that you recognise the best of your writing and cream it off exclusively to share with the world.

Section 3 looks at the community of literature in all its guises, and will help you know where your writing might fit into it. This section provides a starting point for your own research - only you will know which parts need further investigation for you to be able to make the best use of it. Every writer is an amateur - let's say learner - in one aspect or another of the publishing game, because we cannot be all things to all people. The chapters in Section 3 will give you a springboard from which you can dive into the pools that seem most enticing for your line of literary growth.

Read the book from front to back and then keep it to dip into. Certain aspects will become relevant or hit you when writing a particular piece. You'll kick yourself if you can't look again to make sense of it in the light of something you've experienced in your own writing.

Pathways to Publication is an all inclusive title. Finding the right pen, making time to write, getting used to checking your work and improving it, finding a publisher or publishing yourself: all are part of the process. The harder you work, the luckier you'll become.

Section One

You want to be a Writer?

Of course you do, why would you want to be anything else? With that question out of the way this book does little more than offer comfort and support. It will not solve your obsession although it does indicate possible pathways. You may have many reasons for wanting to write, our hope is that you write for yourself. Nobody else really matters.

That said we assume that one eventual aim is for the writer to reach a reader. Showing writers how that can be achieved is a primary objective of author.co.uk and of this book. To satisfy the reader the writer must work steadily through a number of processes. Underlying all that is written here will be the intention of producing a book, one that will be read by someone other than its creator. These pages will follow a central pathway but will allow deviation - plenty of it - as you and other writers contribute, as different styles of writing and of presentation are all examined. Your latest project will never end.

The Start

Let's start at an end. One aim may be to produce a book; just an ink-smeared-on-dead-trees book. Whatever process is finally chosen, the production of the final book must be as good as can be achieved. It's not just about content, which must always be subjected to close scrutiny by a disinterested third party, preferably a professional editor or proof-reader, but also the physical quality of the work.

Unless a book looks and feels good, with a well designed cover, the correct choice of paper, of font and of page layout, it will fail. No matter how good the content. There remains a prejudice against self-published work that can only be overcome by ensuring that the standards of preparation and presentation are rigorously maintained. For too long badly produced booklets, with mono-spaced type, smudged photocopy and bent staples hanging onto a flimsy card cover have dominated the image. That must stop.

In the production process many obstacles have to be overcome but unless the work itself is relevant to an audience no amount of colour, graphic design, expensive paper or hand-crafted binding will hide egotistical, crass or illiterate words on a page.

Being honest to yourself is vital, and the questions asked must be truthfully tackled. What is most important to you? Consider that question carefully, before jumping on a plane to Honolulu with your lover. How will you accomplish your aims and objectives with this publication? What are the priorities and what is your relationship to others, to relatives and friends, and to the community at large? How will your ambitions change these relationships? Importantly, consider where your writing fits into the world? What would be missing if it had never existed? What messages do you have?

Why Write?

At author.co.uk we receive many letters and even more emails asking for basic advice about writing and publishing. Each enquiry is different, but there is a thread that connects all of the many answers that could be given. This book is a small attempt to tie these suggestions together, to make something of a catch-all response for those people who want to publish their own work.

Deliberately there is little encouragement for writing and publishing are very hard work, and are not steps to be taken lightly. For the writer it can be particularly difficult as insecurity and doubt lingers behind the need to learn new tricks; those of management and control, production and cost control, marketing and distribution.

You must ask the 'why write' question of yourself and

answer with absolute truthfulness. Why choose to write at all? Why not go watch the television like everyone else. Go find a lover. Go and be something! Why write? Why condemn yourself to loneliness, to a bad back, to hunched shoulders, to frustration and penury?

Take some time to consider that question. Reject any hopes of fame and fortune. That is a dream world as the average writer fails to receive any adequate recompense for their hours of labour. Look instead at more esoteric goals; to explore and perhaps improve yourself, to provide some explanation to others, to reveal a burning passion, just for the love of words or even because it really is so much better than watching TV. All are logical reasons. A good first step to identify your own reasons.

What to Write?

Fact or fiction. The choice is yours, though the distinction is not always clear-cut. Writers using author.co.uk write for many reasons, but the non-fiction work is often strongly biographical or there is a specific subject area that is dear to the heart of the writer. Both forms of non-fiction require creativity, for if they are to work both will demand that the inner soul of the writer is revealed. The writing focus section of this book must be read with that in mind. Writing non-fiction is a creative process.

Then ask yourself one vitally important question. One that must be repeated as you continue to write, 'Who am I writing this book for? Who is the reader intended to be?' Without some understanding of that audience writing becomes a totally self-indulgent activity. That may be the real reason for starting to write, and it may be why you continue to the end of the piece but in the middle is an altruistic passion to share something with the reader.

Mission Statement

Prepare a mission statement that reveals why you want to write. Once the initial thinking is out the way this should probably be your first task. Your dreams and aspirations must be identified and then closely examined. No matter that they cannot easily be achieved. All writers should prepare a mission statement which states in clear unequivocal terms what they want to do, where they want to go, and what they want to accomplish along the way.

Form of Statement

The mission statement should be short, a single paragraph or a simple list. My first stab came up with, 'to achieve immortality' which over-reaches itself slightly but makes sense to me. That statement would be improved if the needs of a wider world were also to be considered. For me, simply to make money is not enough, perhaps should not even be included, for when personal greed takes precedence, non-financial goals can be difficult to identify and the successful writer (however that is defined) is usually concerned with more ethereal concepts than just mere gelt (money). Whatever your approach try to make a simple statement that describes how you feel.

In between the politicians and the best sellers there's an army of people like you and me who write well. We are the ones who can help fill the void, give words to the wordless, power to the inarticulate and provocation where argument needs fuel.

How precious are you with your work? How far will you compromise? How serious are you in pursuing that particular publication?

These are the questions you learn to answer for yourself.

The heart of the matter

These are important questions that take us to the soul of our work. It is easy enough to churn out words but why do we do it? What does it achieve? How does it fit into the world in which we live? Would it be missed if it had never been published?

The Result

So, the mission statement, a few brief yet carefully chosen words that express why we want to publish our work, may help us to find an acceptable perspective.

To allow a start to be made let us assume the concept for the work is already in place. You know what you want to write, even if it is only a simple construct in your mind. The final version is still a long way off. At this stage allow your imagination considerable licence. All is possible. Any journey starts with one small step. The finished work can follow the accepted formats, or can offer some unusual perspectives.

Full-length fiction normally assumes a work stretching beyond 60,000 words, so with about 400 words per typed page there will be over 120 pages in the pile of paper on your desk. Short stories are usually collected together to make a bound work that looks the same as a novel, something over 100 pages. Poetry books are often slimmer, a poem a page with just 30 works in a slim volume makes for a romantic tinge. Works of non-fiction, good and stolid, factually correct are of indeterminate length. They have taken as long as it took the author to explain the subject matter - even though that is often too long, but more of that later.

These are conventions that often remain unstated and are not sacrosanct. It is useful to go to any library or bookshop and look carefully at the books on the shelves. More importantly look at the books that are selling in the bookshops; at those books that people are looking at with interest. Your book could look like those, perhaps it should, whether it will be a suitably acceptable clone, whether it will sell, these are all matters within your control.

You as the Publisher

As a publisher, for in following this book to its conclusion that is what you are about to become, both a published author and a small publisher, you may feel free to experiment with the approach. Try, at this stage, to free your mind from the idea that this manuscript (MS, plural MSS) will pass through the hands of a trade publisher, be printed into a book and be sold through a bookshop. That is only one of several pathways that can be followed.

One author recently published the first chapter of her forthcoming novel as a short story, in the form of a small booklet. From this the reader gained an idea of the writing style, the characters and plot. The titles of subsequent chapters were shown, with pertinent sub-headings, to encourage the reader to fill in the order form at the back of the booklet and actually buy the completed novel. This order form included details of several other titles as well. The author was gaining Brownie points at every turn. She gained money for a short story that would form part of a novel and also provided advertising for the larger work, and promoting other books at the same time. Such thinking at an early stage can prove useful.

Electronic Publishing

Electronic publishing is already beginning to demonstrate its potential and versatility. Undoubtedly it will provide new opportunities, as also will short-run printing methods, multi-media projects and audio presentations. Your words could end up just about anywhere. For now, let them just arrive like the fresh growth of a glorious Spring day.

It is this lack of lateral format that makes author-publishing so exciting for the writer. Modern trade publishers are constricted by the need to make money, and to disregard any other reason for bringing a creative work to the attention of a wider public. They forget about ideas, about breaking new ground.

Tools of the Trade

Publishing today means using computers, digital wonders of this new age. They are a necessary tool for every writer who must become intimately involved with this pliable plastic demon for it heralds a revolution that transcends the invention of the printing press. One dire word of warning - when discarding one haggard heap of a machine and moving on to the keys of a new darling do remember to make back-up copies of your old work in the new medium. I once had 8" disks on my Wang word-processor, others had 3" Amstrads, many of us used CPM before DOS, which Windows has now overtaken, and Apple refused for years to talk to Bill Gates. People find comfort in Unix and Linux and there are other systems lurking in corners.

The disks, the drives, the software and the machines are all constantly disappearing, like box cameras and black and white TV's, as new technology appears. So as you move on down these new super highways, just remember to take all your material with you, like an old tramp on the road. Back-up tapes do not last forever, and no-one yet really knows how long a CD-ROM will last. If in doubt, take a paper copy on acid free paper! Although even that will give no guarantee on the longevity of the toner or ink used by your printer. Just be aware that computers can store material very well, but disks need to be used if they are to retain their magnetism and copies need to be taken when moving to new equipment.

Preservation

This is not to labour the point but a few years ago I gave evidence to a government inquiry about the preservation of electronic materials. That report is gathering dust somewhere in the National Preservation Office (there's a name to conjure with) but the issues raised remain important.

The report produced by our hours of deliberation suggested standards should be set for the archiving of digital material. The National Office of Digital Archiving (NODA) would be responsible for developing standards and guidelines for archiving digital materials. The job of maintaining the archives should be contracted out to specialist agencies with the appropriate expertise. Once material is selected for preservation it should be kept for ever (whatever that means). It said that funding for digital archiving must come from the public sector via higher education institutions, legal deposit libraries, the funding councils and NODA itself. Legal deposit legislation should be amended to cover electronic publications and other digital material such as sound and video recordings.

Nothing seems to have happened since except that it made me realise how much I have lost over the years, and extrapolating that idea can lead to a vision that shows the loss of our entire civilisation. Switch off the electricity as you leave the planet and then ask yourself what happened to those travellers known as Homo sapiens.

What to Do?

One of the first jobs to undertake having bought a new computer must be to transfer all existing files to the new machine. If you change to a new word-processing program make sure that the old material can be accessed. It's probably a good idea to ensure that all your files can be read by at least two programs, even if one of those is just a simple text editor like Notepad.

Floppy disks hold information using magnetism. Who knows how that works? We do know that floppy disks can lose the magnetic charge and so make it impossible to read the files they contain. Check floppy disks regularly, just inserting them into a drive may be enough to recharge their will to live.

CD-ROMS, tape drives, zip drives and hard disks are all great places to store data but try to save your beloved words in more than one format.

Printing?

By now Luddites will be applauding my cynicism; believing it reinforces their belief in the fragility, nay instability, of computers. Unfortunately printing everything out need not be much better. Most of the paper we use is acidic, and will decay within a few years. Many of the printers attached to PC's rely upon magnetism, so printed pages carefully placed into a filing cabinet and left for several decades will probably turn to yellowed paper surrounded by graphite dust formed as your words slid from the page when gravity beat magnetism.

Writing

Despite the present difficulty of ensuring the longevity of digital material, it is clear that preparing shaky script with a pencil for a typist to translate is no longer really feasible. Every writer must learn to use a word processor of some sort. You already know that, you have Internet access. You are one of the elite.

The creative potential available through using computers is incredible. Most word processing programs have facilities that most writers will never learn to use, which is a great pity. The limit has now really been reached, if you just want a substitute typewriter, with an upmarket duplicator - then any of today's PC's together with a good ink-jet or laser printer will handle all you need - except you will want more!

Word Processing

Spelling Checkers

Everyone should understand how to use the word processor's spelling checker and the thesaurus, remembering that both can be improved. Programs can be purchased to increase the number of words in the computer's dictionary, and do make use of the facility that allows a special dictionary to be created. Grammar can also be edited using computer programs, some of these are very helpful, but the use of a real-person editor or proofreader remains essential. Grammar checkers can give some valuable advice and those giving a 'readability factor' do point you in the right direction. There is no point using language that your audience will not find comfortable. Ensure that the correct language is used. English is not a single entity; it may be UK British in style, or English-American, or English-International or any one of a myriad variety. There is a growing difference!

Moving and Marking Text

The word-processing program allows the creation of Tables of Content, indexes or lists, even a Table of Authorities, footnotes, endnotes, annotations and cross references. It will probably allow you to produce an outline, an invaluable tool for many writers, as it allows sections of text to be identified by using an explanatory word or phrase. The outline can be printed at intervals and kept beside the writer as they work. Particular subjects can be quickly found, and sections easily moved within the document. The ability to move, re-order and change blocks of text is absolutely invaluable and is a major reason why all writers should use computers.

Production

Increasingly the writer is becoming involved with the production process, whether or not they decide to publish their own work. No longer are ragged bundles of hand-written foolscap tied with ribbon stuck in the garret of a publisher's office. Now writers tend to present their work on computer disk, prepared using a standard word processing package. The work will then have to be edited, proofread and marked up ready for printing. Many commercial printing companies now print straight from a computer disk supplied by the writer.

A Writer's Bookshelf

Your bookshelf should contain: a good dictionary; a Thesaurus, and Roget still holds sway; The Writers Handbook or The Writers and Artists Yearbook; 'The Elements of Style' by Strunk & White; 'Cassell Guide to Common Errors in English' by Harry Blamires; Eric Partridge's 'Usage & Abusage' and 'You have a point there'. Get plenty of reference books, buy secondhand books on any subject and new books on the subject of your latest project. A fiction writer needs books on the weather, on antiques, flowers, furniture, birds, trees. 'Right Word, Wrong Word' V H Collins (Longman) Brewer's Dictionary of Phrase and Fable is a useful addition to the collection. A concise dictionary of English Slang, the Book of Days and a Dictionary of Dates can all be found space on your book shelf.

Bits & Pieces

A Tape Recorder

Or a dictaphone are very useful for some purposes. Use them to record interviews, argue with yourself, to sort out dialogue or to make quick notes in the strangest places. Tom Sharpe is reported to have had a typewriter in every room in his house, including the loo, ready to capture a fleeting idea.

Paper

A4 is the paper size these days in Europe, America still uses the Letter size. Make sure your computer default uses the right size. Quality is another thing. Use cheap copier paper for draft work, go upmarket when submitting material.

Envelopes

A4 for MSS, the self-stick variety are only marginally more expensive but much easier on the tongue. Save on coffee and orange juice, buy self -stick. Did you know that licking a postage stamp can add 8 calories to your body? Slimmers beware!

Paper Clips et al

Get some giant paper clips, they hold MSS together and look so good on your desk. Make sure you have a serviceable desk, and proper chair. You will be sitting there for hours once you start writing. Add a good pair of long scissors, a two-hole punch and a stapler. Consider buying a long-reach stapler that will make it easy to make booklets by folding a few sheets of A4 in half (to make A5), wrapping a cardboard cover around them, two staples in the centre fold - makes one booklet. Document folders, plastic envelopes, even cardboard boxes for cuttings and other useful background material junk. A secondhand filing cabinet can be an invaluable investment, providing the dining room/office/bedroom can stand its appearance. Mine has some glass vases and a plant sitting on a large lace runner. It doesn't hide it, just makes everyone believe that it's accepted. They seem to believe it should be there or at least they make no comment.

Computer software

Is another ball-game. MS Word is slowly becoming a de facto standard. You may not like its intrusive nature, but it is widely available. Take care when sending such files as attachments to emails as they are very easily attacked by viruses. One day perhaps Microsoft will tackle the problem but unfortunately that company has very many enemies, and having achieved phenomenal growth has not taken time to step back and examine its own concepts and rationale in any depth. It has made huge amounts of money, and achieved massive control over many of our lives. It should also accept responsibility.

The reality is that any word-processing program will do the job. If all else fails save your files to ASCII or RTF (Rich Text Format) which is normally readable by most computers.

Whichever program you use, get to love and understand

it - it is superbly flexible and powerful. If it doesn't work, the chances are it is your fault! At least you will be forced to rely on your own devices as the company providing the program is unlikely to allow you to talk to a real person who understands your problem.

Beyond Word Processing

Just bear in mind that once you have mastered word-processing and made sure your printer works well then will come the scanner, more software to create multi-media packages; such as Adobe Acrobat and Macromedia Director and Web design packages to allow you to create your own web site.

These days a writer cannot expect much from publishers. Most productive writers know at least something about the processes of production and of marketing and promotion.

Take time to understand

Time spent understanding your computer programs will be well-spent. There is appalling ignorance out there - and as a result many writers miss many opportunities.

There are a bewildering variety of other programs, plug-ins and other devices promoted to writers. Most do their job well enough but they can waste more time than they save. Recently we have seen a number of programs that purport to help the creative writer, with plot and character creation. I remain unconvinced that a computer program can do much to help the creative writer but some may help.

Just as interesting are the random word generators, poetry programs, anagram makers and more. Many are available as free downloads, so why not try them and see? Do make sure they are properly installed on your machine as that should ensure they can be deleted from your system when they become redundant.

Author Interviews

Over the years I have talked to many thousands of writers. Too often I've talked *at* them and have not always listened to them carefully enough. It was time to introduce a little structure and so began a short series of interviews with authors that were intended to discover what made them tick, and whether they could provide any useful tips or pointers for budding writers.

Raymond Chandler is alleged to have suggested that trying to help new writers was a waste of time. I disagree with that sentiment, as there is always something to be gained from the experience of others, and why should we expect each new generation to invent their own version of a wheel when the basic outline plans already exist. There are many 'wannabees' out there; folk who will never become writers. They are the reason for the peremptory 'no unsolicited MSS' often broadcast by publishers and agents. There are too many literary agents pretentiously dismissing new writers, but that's another story.

New writers are not really the heart of the problem rather it is the system that can only measure success in terms of money and fame. Competitions abound, magazines, books and directories of contacts all suggest that international recognition means success. Too few of us will ever realise those dreams and the publishing industry, as a whole, needs to address these issues in radical ways but these interviews with a small selection of authors give some indicators that will prove useful. Most published authors make very little money from their labours and if an hourly rate were calculated legal action for underpayment would result.

Susan Perry

The authors interviewed this year were not chosen with any especial care, most just arrived on the doorstep by chance. They are not representative although I did interview Susan

Perry, a California-based writer who obtained a doctorate by interviewing and analysing 75 well-known American writers and one Dutchman. Her 'Writing in Flow' theory says that you will enter and stay in flow if you're intrinsically motivated to do a thing, and if you obtain sufficient feedback to encourage you to continue. She says writers have to learn how to give themselves that necessary feedback. Each writer she interviewed had a different method. Often they shared the work with others, something that beginners find difficult or they choose an inappropriate mentor, such as a spouse or friend.

Susan Perry believes writing is important for at least two reasons. First; to relieve us of some festering ideas, thoughts, and emotions; or to leave something behind, communicating something to others. There is a cathartic process in writing, perhaps a diary or a just a series of letters. It can be very helpful emotionally. It can even relieve physical symptoms. Simply expressing oneself is a good thing for the individual. We also owe it to future generations to leave behind some record of our lives.

Josie Lloyd & Emlyn Rees

One of the early interviews this year was with Josie Lloyd and Emlyn Rees. Initially they had started writing together as something of a joke. Their friendship had developed into a marriage and our meeting was enlivened by the gurgles and cries of their new baby. Writing in partnership is unusual and they had really broken new ground by writing with two distinct voices. The partnership had not always run smoothly, they had thrown away large chunks of text because both of them had to be completely content before anything was included. That Emlyn had worked for the literary agents, Curtis Brown, who had just started to look after Josie's writing career provided yet another clue to success. It does help to know someone in the business. Jane Tatam of Amolibros, a lady with considerable publishing experience has researched this subject and concluded that practically all of the top-rank writers achieved success as a result of someone they knew in a publishing company or they obtained that vital first step from someone with similarly good contacts.

David Lodge

David Lodge had taken another, more conventional, route. An academic, his novels and writing style reflect the world in which he lives. Three novels were turned down before he found a publisher. His early novel, Changing Places, was the turning point in his writing career. It was well received and has now sold over 400,000 copies His stance was that persistence is required, and quality will eventually succeed. Whether that is quite as true today as when he first gained success in 1975 is questionable.

He believes the creative writing courses now offered by many universities may improve but can never make a writer. Courses, such as that at the University of East Anglia masterminded by the late Malcolm Bradbury have been a stunning success, particularly as they now attract high-quality students and can be selective. Perhaps it is time to measure the success of such academic courses, but how will that be measured?

Joy Larkcom

Two fiction writers had me turning to more prosaic arenas. Where better for a foodie like me to visit than the home of Joy Larkcom, the doyen of the potager, supreme champion of the vegetable garden. Her first book, Oriental Vegetables, was the culmination of ten years research. Here was an expert pouring out mountains of information, assisted by publishers willing to stand the cost of printing expensive four-colour books. Writers need to consider the means of production, especially the cost of printing in full colour. Indeed writers must become professional in their approach to the business if they are to succeed. That was a precept that was already becoming clear as I interviewed writers. In Joy's case her books needed full-colour printing to display all those lovely vegetables, which in turn meant long print runs; the large quantities of books being printed during one print run reducing the cost of each individual book but bringing extra risk for the publisher. It's no coincidence that big, glossy books are often found in bookshops selling remaindered books (copies of books publishers have sold off cheaply once they have satiated the conventional market). Pity the publisher deciding to print 30,000 copies of a book. Who will buy? One major publisher was brought to its knees last year by over-printing too many copies of one book.

Talking to Joy Larkcom highlighted several factors. First; non-fiction books account for 80% of the books published in most years. Secondly; there is a steady market for books by experts, but don't expect to get rich quick and also that the writer must consider the whole publishing process. Joy was first in her field with her books. She knew her subject and the publisher had faith. However she could not rely upon books alone to pay the bills. She was luckier than most as she could put food on the table by growing it herself.

Ian Rankin

Ian Rankin was next in line and I was surprised by the similarities to be found comparing a crime writer like Ian with the non-fiction writer Joy Larkcom. They were both writing about something they knew and loved. For Ian that was his native city, the Scottish capital of Edinburgh, and with one main character, Inspector Rebus. Ian is a writer's writer. He is an exemplar for us all. He began his writing career at four years of age. Clearly scribbling was in his blood, practically an obsession. By the time he went to university he described himself as a poet. Wanting to enter a competition he became a short story writer. He won the competition. One of his short stories afterwards became his first book, Flood, written in 1986.

Once again we see dedication, total absorption and self-belief. Ian urges all writers to believe in themselves and to enter competitions and prizes and to submit ideas and book proposals to suitable publishers.

This professional approach and knowledge of his subject has worked for Ian. He has won prizes and plaudits, with the biggest breakthrough coming in 1994 with the award of a Crime Writers Association Short Story Dagger, then another in 1996, and in 1997 he received the CWA Gold Dagger Award for the best crime novel of the year for Black & Blue.

Zeal and determination clearly lay behind Ian's success, and incidentally a willing and supportive partner. It was Ian's wife that persuaded him to take a year in France to write a novel. He would not have done that without her support.

Julian Stockwin

Successful partnerships were beginning to be a factor in my search for the Writers Grail. The next interview reinforced that assertion. Julian Stockwin is my age and that means he is definitely getting on a bit. Having spent a lifetime in the navy upon his retirement he started to write software programs. At the conclusion of one long contract he was so exhausted by the effort that his lovely wife, Kathy, told him to stop such nonsense, promising to support him while he wrote his first book.

This clever and organised pair did more than write a book, they planned a series of books, not presenting themselves to Carole Blake, one of the best literary agents, until Julian was halfway through the second book in the series. Carole showed how useful an agent can be, quickly realising she had been presented with an expert in naval history who could write a good yarn. Here was a recognisable genre that had a willing, but knowledgeable, audience. The leading writer in this field had died recently leaving a chasm that needed to be filled. She quickly found two publishers willing to take the book. That's a wonderful situation for an agent to find for herself as an auction began with the highest bidder walking off with Julian Stockwin, author. Julian signed a lucrative contract to supply four books, one a year. That is a good situation for both writer and publisher. They have a measure of security and the publisher is more willing to invest in a long-term prospect.

George Szirtes

George Szirtes is a respected poet and translator. Born in Hungary he now lives in Norfolk and is an established member of the British writing scene. Together with Penelope Lively he judged the British Council's 'New Writing 10' the latest of a yearly collection of new writing from the UK and Commonwealth. New writing did not mean new writers and the criteria of selection remains unclear. George had felt it necessary to include some translations. This year an Irishman and a Scotsman will have selected the pieces. Will they display any bias?

There are a considerable number of bursaries, fellowships, grants and prizes available. Close examination will reveal that many writers are excluded from these pots of gold. Too often only published authors can apply or the submissions must come from recognised publishers. More frustratingly prizes are awarded for lifetime achievement, and so the money ends up in the bank accounts of those who probably have more than enough already. The important function of these prizes and awards is the publicity they can generate; for the writer, for writing, reading and for the sponsors.

Geoff Pridmore

Writers can find markets if they search assiduously enough. Geoff Pridmore believes many writers should consider becoming freelance journalists as magazines and newspapers are cutting back on staff so giving far more opportunities for freelancers. At the time of our interview during the Winchester Writers' Weekend he had just completed his book, 'Journalism', which has a large section containing interviews with journalists, each describing how they obtained work. Geoff's own experience of finding a book publisher showed, once again, that a professional approach works.

He approached Hodder & Stoughton with a proposal for one book about theatre in education. The publisher rejected that idea but asked if he could write a Teach Yourself Theatre book. This time it was Geoff who felt he could not cope with such a project but by then the publisher was hooked, returning to suggest he write the book about journalism. It was clear that the publisher recognised Geoff as a professional and was prepared to accept him as one of their authors.

Sandi Toksvig

Is our very own Danish comedian. 'Flying Under Bridges' is her second book for adults, she has written several more for children. She says authors must stand back from what they do, that the whole point of writing is to escape to somewhere else. You must know about locations, sensations but the characters in the book are not real. Her first book dealt with the emerging issues of womens' liberation, this latest work is about the kind of morality preached by the tabloid press and politicians. She does not believe that the country, as a whole, adheres to that sort of nonsense. Her reaction is to point a comical finger at the hacks, to peel away the layers to reveal hypocrisy.

She loves writing more than anything else, and would love to be doing it all the time. There is no money in it and so she must continue to do something else, anything to bring in funds to maintain her new home and look after her children, whom she clearly adores.

Sandi Toksvig is a disciplined person. Her writing regime for a book starts with intensive research, hundreds of pages of notes before she begins to start writing the novel. On a writing day she does just that. Gets up, starts writing, stops for lunch, writes more. Although the novel may take 18 months to complete that is not a true reflection of the speed in which she writes. Her brain is sharp, talking to her you know she has considered the question, run through the consequences of possibilities and formulated an answer before your lips have stopped moving. Her world is fast, and that shows in her writing.

She suggests that writing is like practising the piano. It is something you must do every day. Work at it until it comes right. It's no good waiting for the Muse or seeking inspiration in a whisky tumbler. Work at it.

John Hegley

John Hegley is our best-known performance poet. He tours the country with his show, at which he also tries to sell his books of poetry. This is not an easy area but John shows that an audience can be found. His income comes from several sources, and like many writers he cannot rely upon writing alone to support his lifestyle. He urges poets not to be discouraged believing that publishing your own work was a good way to explore markets and bring work to public notice. John has produced several small volumes of his own, often experimenting with new approaches. Book covers have varied; one book covered in sandpaper, another wrapped in carpet.

Durlabh Singh

Durlabh Singh was a civil servant, painter and poet. For much of his life work has subsidised his art. Now retired through ill-health he has embraced the Internet, posting examples of his work on several Web sites. He survives by drawing income from many sources; teaching poetry courses, selling his paintings from exhibitions with a small sum coming from writing.

Durlabh's experience is not uncommon. The Society of Authors stated recently that the average income of full-time writers was under £5,000 per year. The reality behind such statistics may be that a few writers make plenty of money, while the rest make very little. That doesn't stop them scribbling and trying to bring their efforts to public notice.

Margot Strickland

The most inspirational writer I interviewed during the year was Margot Strickland. Once an actress she turned to writing by producing a biography of her cousin, the concert pianist Maura. Today she writes plays; beautifully constructed pieces written by a professional who understands what will work in the theatre. She not only writes the plays, she then hires a theatre, producing the whole event herself; hiring a director, selecting suitable actors, advertising and promoting and supervising the entire event. She is an inspiration and an example to us all. Don't just sit there bemoaning at the lack of response from unsuitable publishers. Do it yourself. A selection of Margot's plays will soon be published using our print on demand service.

John Spurling

John Spurling is another playwright with over twenty-five plays to his credit. We experimented with a selection of his play scripts at author.co.uk making these available as free downloads in Adobe Acrobat. We believe a play does not spring to life until it is performed, so the script can be given away provided those wishing to perform the plays pay John for the right to perform his work. We still don't know if this is an appropriate action but it is a step forward and may prove worthwhile.

John Dawes

There is one writer to blame for my involvement in writing and publishing. John Dawes persuaded me to join him in writing and publishing our first book twenty years ago. At that time he was putting together a comprehensive guide to the planning and construction of swimming pools. Not that he knew much about pools but he wanted to build one in the garden of his new house but could not find a suitable book on the subject, so he wrote one. The Design and Planning of Swimming Pools resulted and remains today the industry standard on the subject. He published the book himself having discovered that he knew more about the subject than any publisher. That approach has worked well, and John Dawes is just one example of hundreds of writers I know who have written and successfully published books in specialist areas.

Jancis Robinson

Jancis Robinson became one of Britain's best-known writers on wine largely by default. She was one of the few women jobbing journalists writing about wine when a friend asked why she hadn't written a book. She submitted a synopsis to an agent, who promptly sold the book to that same friend, who was a publisher! That started her along a road where she has only ever responded to requests, or demands, placed upon her by others. Unusually she has never originated another project. Each book has been prompted by suggestions from publishers and agents. At least that's the way Jancis tells the story. The reality is rather different. Here is another very professional writer, confident in her abilities and willing to take chances. It was her own money behind her very successful television series about wine. She is now the editor of the World Atlas of Wine.

Freddy Macha

I have saved my interview with Freddy Macha until last because it gave me the most pleasure. We met at a workshop organised by the National Association of Writers in Education where Freddy had all the delegates moving round in a circle making music and building a collective word poem. We met again at the launch of his CD, Kiliminjaro, at Momo's, an Algerian restaurant in London. Freddy is an enthusiastic teacher, whose poetry bites home. His words, which are often set to music showed me a new dimension and made clear the delight we can all obtain by living in a truly multi-cultural environment. Spending time with Freddy and his beautiful wife makes me zing with the pleasure of living in England, a land whose people willingly embrace all those who are prepared to proffer their own friendship.

Conclusions

All of these writers are professionals. They write good books but that is not all. They know their subjects and their business, and all work tirelessly to maintain a network of contacts. 'Better the Devil you know' rings very true in every case. It may be there are plenty of writers out there just as competent, compelling and informative as this motley collection but my interviewees have all exploited their own world with enthusiasm and dedication that has produced results. They are all professionals.

Diaries and Journals

All writers should keep some form of diary or journal. They are the start of the process of being a writer.

Even if you don't know 'famous' writers for their novels or factual writings, you will probably have read or heard extracts from their diaries. You might think there is nothing special enough about *your* life that's worth recording, but think again. You've probably got more profound things to say than all the celebrities, often non-writers, whose memoirs are piled high in the bookshops.

Ordinary life is the main ingredient for every work of fiction, and the ability to put detail, explanation and subtlety into any piece of writing, hinges on the skill of interpreting actions into words on the page. The expertise is gained through practice. Even if the diaries you write never come to anything more than practice, you will gain a great deal by writing them.

Other People's Diaries

Look at www.diarist.net to find a registry of links to numerous diarists' entries, in which ordinary people write their own online diaries on their free web space; and register it to link with Diarist.net. These diaries take many forms, from poetic exposition through personal experiences to love letters. There are personal viewpoints from, for example, expectant surrogate mothers: if you can find a diarist writing about your specialist interest, then reading these diaries can be the very best research for your own writing.

Write about yourself

There is no doubt that writing about yourself can help to define who you are by outlining your beliefs and what you want to do with your life. This may demand an honesty that you have not needed previously in your life. Your mind will become focused and it will bring peace and organisation to your life.

Writing a diary will sort out problems, collect ideas together, organise your life and offer a sanctuary from the chaos that surrounds you in the life outside of your diary. In these writing focus pages you'll find that personal writing is of the utmost importance in finding your voice and your style in being a writer.

Your diary will become an uncritical 'shoulder to rely upon', allowing your inner mind to express itself more clearly. Look at the positive and joyful parts of your life examining what makes you really happy.

As the years roll by the diary will provide a record of your life, an aide-memoir for clarity, a record of events and of tasks you have accomplished. It will show that your life has not been wasted. It will show patterns of events in your own life and will surprise you when you look back to discover a certain thing happened to you within the same week as a world event was taking place.

Making you a better person

A diary will help you to communicate more effectively, because it is practice in putting words to something that might be incomprehensible to other people. As a spin-off it will serve as a family history for future generations to enjoy.

The diarist site is excellent and has some great suggestions for techniques that can be adopted when writing a diary. You'll find some of these suggestions familiar in further writing focus pages and you might like to consider :

Freewriting

Put pen to paper to write everything that comes to your mind. Don't stop to correct or read what you've written. Keep going, mistakes, rubbish and all for 10 to 30 minutes.

Focused Freewriting

Pick a topic before you begin and try to write everything that comes into your mind about that topic. Write for at least ten minutes.

Brainstorming

Draw a shape (such as a box, oval, or circle) in the middle of a blank page and write the topic you wish to write about inside it. Draw lines branching off from your topic, ending with more shapes, each filled with sub-topics relating to the main topic. Some people have called it a 'Starburst' of ideas. There are mind mapping programs that will help achieve the same task. The programs often allow even more free expression than paper and pencil.

Writing Prompts

Use a word bowl or a list of questions to spark ideas. A word bowl is a container full of words that you've cut out of magazines, or slips of paper you've written words on.

Ask someone else to give you a word or theme to get you going. The 'distance' of someone else's perspective can provide you with an unusual freedom.

Making Lists

Makes you only consider specific topics. Expansion is then easier, next time you come to write.

Descriptive Writing

Involves writing in vivid detail how you perceive the world around you. Write from your point of view. Sit down with a pen and pad and write what you see, just as an artist might set up easel and paint the landscape before him.

Portraits

Capture another person on paper: their personality, mannerisms, opinions, relationship to you. Describe facial expressions and the way these change when they feel cold, miserable, happy, excited, et al.

Reflective Writing

Pause after several weeks of writing to reflect on your past thoughts and actions, and consider your future. If a diary is to be for self examination it's important to write down how you *feel* about events.

Altered Point of View

Try putting yourself in someone else's shoes. Change sex, or become the omnipotent third party. This can really be quite an eye-opener, and will certainly make you a better person in that you'll be able to empathize with those around you.

However much you try to write a total fiction, there will always be an element of yourself, your hopes and fears, within the pages. Don't fight it. Your experience is good; and contrary to what you might think, if it came from the bottom of your heart then it will meet with your readers' minds where it matters.

Meditative Writing

Be very relaxed and clear your mind of all thoughts. This is meditation. Use an image to create fantasy, think upon the tranquil, serene or peaceful. Or you may be able to draw a picture, from intuition, drawing without thinking of what you are doing. Doodling is a version of this but instead of doodling while you talk on the phone or listen to a lecture, try doodling to simply fill a blank page. By the time the page is filled, your mind will be buzzing with ideas worth writing.

Intensive Writing

Writing can be a cathartic process, clearing out all the rubbish in your mind to produce clarity and peace. Highly emotional writing that is freely expressed but really says what you want to say. Scream at the page as you write.

Dialogue

Conduct a conversation in writing, representing both points of view. Talk to yourself, apparently George Sand did.

Unsent Letters

Another way of clearing out the detritus in your mind, to tell someone how it really is, in writing, knowing that you will not send it. No need to be polite, to consider feelings - just sock it to them!

Radio Diaries

The www.radiodiaries.org site says: 'Radio can be a lot of things: Radio can be a news report. Radio can be a commentary. Radio can be a conversation. Radio can be an audio postcard. Your story can be a combination of all this and more.'

They provide lots of good information and advice to help use this medium. Well worth a visit.

Talking into a tape recorder is very different to writing, and you might baulk at the thought. However, you'll be surprised at what comes out of your head when you get used to talking to yourself.

Try keeping an audio journal. Start by sending tapes to a distant friend. It can be an electronic diary. Start with yourself then talk to your family and your friends; ask them to tell their stories. The statesman Tony Benn has used this to record every event in his life and now has an enormous collection of tapes.

Very quickly you will be sticking the microphone under all sorts of noses - and finding that people are quite happy to answer your questions, often very frankly.

Soon you could be making radio documentaries, letting the audience participate and experience things as they happen, and carrying your tape recorder wherever you go - like a press photographer and reporter, ready to record events as they happen.

Most of the information in this section has come from the www.radiodiaries.org site

Journals versus Diaries

Whereas a diary is thought of as a regular record (and consequently sometimes mundane), a journal is an occasional occupation. You write up an entry in your journal whenever you feel like putting something into words. It might be an observation you want to remember, or an occasion that deserves recording in complete detail.

Your journal entry will be more thoughtful and more discursive than a regular diary. Listen to (or read) the Diaries of Alan Bennett. He records all sorts of observations, and frequently admits his feelings about what he has seen. His accounts of a day with his mother are every bit as interesting as his meeting famous actors and directors, because he reveals what the rest of us might say about our own circumstances.

Diaries and journals keep you in the habit of writing and are a constant way of teaching yourself to write. Sooner or later the completed diary will be opened again and its subjects aired within the pages of your fiction or your documentary.

Audio Diaries are similarly useful as time goes on. A writer must seek detail to make the work seem authentic, and sometimes the detail of a private life can only be found in a diary.

Learning to write

Diaries and journals are an excellent starting point. Keep a freewriting notebook and take it anywhere, everywhere.

Keep a diary of special events, holidays, and hectic days when it will be useful to reap hindsight of the way events unfolded. By their very nature, daily diary entries are subtle in the telling, yet lively and concise. Reading them later will reveal secret crevices.

Record your dreams and your maddest ideas because they, too, will become useful in your writing.

One of the greatest ways to start feeling confident as a writer is to record your thoughts on how your writing feels to you, and monitoring - in words on the page - how you progress. As your writing career develops, so will your appreciation of your collection of diaries and journals that are loaded with meaningful source material.

Therapy

It could be said that all writing is therapy. Whether you write about your problems, or write something completely distant from your experience, the act of writing is like an elixir. This magic potion might seem like medicine, but it won't necessarily be a cure for all ills. You have to do it for yourself to find out.

Don't worry about spelling and grammar

There are enough internal and external censors without the mechanics of writing getting in the way. Let computers, dictionaries, grammar checks and a thesaurus do that, much later. For now, just write - anything that is in your head.

Privacy

Make sure you are away from others, with nobody looking over your shoulder, with the risk of interruptions at a minimum. Sitting in the park or in a vehicle can be ideal. It doesn't have to be for long, five minutes can yield 200 words or more when you've got something to express. When you haven't, try 'automatic' writing, mentioned in Diaries (as Freewriting) and also in Visualise.

Ways to Avoid Embarrassment

Even if you have no trauma to exorcise, it can be hard to show your feelings in words, and even harder to see them yourself, let alone let others see them.

> Disguise yourself by writing as if this were not you, but someone wearing a bright red coat or a hat made of green leather.

> Write in third person. Did you just flush the loo and open the curtains? Write: He flushed the toilet and went to open the long blue curtains, letting in daylight -

Write in metaphors. You fell out with your best friend? No, you severed the flower head. Will you be able to make it up again? Perhaps: the cut was below a leaf joint so a new root might just grow. Continue the metaphorical story . . .

Write a symbolic account. The love affair is over but it was great while it lasted: the cruise ship pulled out of harbour and the adventures on board began. The end of the journey is the end of your story.

Stand Back

Put a distance between yourself and your writing. Distance means time as well as space. When you walk away from it, you remember what else you could have written. You can go back to it with a freshness that would have eluded you if you'd stuck at it for too long. The funny thing is, if the writing is your therapy, then standing back means you'll bound into a fresh mind-set after every spurt of work.

Give your experiences shape

One of the hardest things about life is making sense of it as you go along. Writing about your experiences, whether in disguise or as a plain diary or journal, will show you some truths about yourself. What are your goals in life? What stands in the way? The answers to how to stop these conflicts may inadvertently come through and hit you between the eyes. See Get a Life! for some suggestions on solving problems.

Understand Your Friends and Relatives

In the same way, writing about past experiences will reveal shape and meaning that you never thought existed. It might even cause you to act on a forgotten (or nagging) piece of unfinished business.

The Heart of Good Writing

Writing Therapy is a stepping stone to writing good prose - fact or fiction - because the writer must connect with the reader. When you write for personal therapeutic reasons you're practising a skill that could take years of academic tuition to achieve, and still the important 'melting point' with the reader might elude you.

The best writers share what is in their heart as well as what's in their head.

If you're looking for a writing course that accentuates the value of writing from the heart, go to Writing Life® at www.writinglife.org.uk

Take a Life - any life, and consider it from different angles.

"Men are disturbed not by things, but by the view they take of them."
~ Epictetus, Greek philosopher AD 55 -135.

Grouching Therapy

Of all the different types of writers in the world, one thing above all unites us: the need to be heard. We want some recognition. This chapter assumes you are already writing and sending your work to publishers in the hope of becoming a successful author. It resides near the start of our creative writing section, because many writers feel at ease with non-fiction; and by sending articles to a variety of destinations, you glean confidence before embarking on a longer work of fiction. If you're not yet sending off your work to prospective publishers this chapter will show how accommodating you might need to become.

Article writing is valuable for learning to meet the needs of potential readers. You might feel you are regarded as creative one minute and a jobbing writer the next. Doing anything to obtain a living wage. It's a lonely job, though, and we're all sensitive to the way our 'babies' are handled. It's therapeutic to talk about it and to hear others' experiences.

Whichever way you do it, writing - and getting those words noticed - is hard; but for all that you also need to consider the task of the editor or publisher - we are all human. Remember editors are writers too. It is vital to have empathy with readers, and that means your work must first pluck a chord with the editor.

What to Expect?

If you're a trained journalist you'll know how much of your copy might be changed, censored, or cropped to suit the readership. You will have learned to see good work cut, and will know what level of alteration is acceptable to you.

If you're a specialist writer - chosen for publication because of the knowledge you can impart - then you can set reasonably strict boundaries. If you're wise, you'll know the editor is always right. If you're on the best terms, you can discuss, not dispute.

Creative writers who are trying to earn a crust have to learn by listening and trusting their hearts. Your mistakes are your best teachers. Here are some writers' experiences from which you may glean insight, ideas, hope or succour.

From a specialist writer:

"There was a new editor and I was commissioned to write a double-page spread about my subject, on top of my long-standing regular series. I sent it off in good time, its arrival was acknowledged; but a day before the publication was due to go to press, I received the galley proof. This was most unusual - my copy was normally accepted and planted straight into the magazine verbatim. I looked closer and found that three of the headings and whole paragraphs had been changed - offering totally wrong, inappropriate advice.

"I hadn't found my letters until mid-afternoon so it was in shock and panic that I phoned the editor - who was conveniently absent. Speaking to the sub-editor I realised that saying 'why?' wasn't the way forward. I suggested I rewrite those paragraphs, to be more in keeping with what the new editor evidently envisaged, agreeing a very short deadline - next day I think. Failing that, I said, the article would have to go under a pen name as I couldn't possibly endorse the new editor's advice. I wracked my brains and supplied fresh copy, so all was well. I could only thank the sub-editor for her unusual action in sending the galley proof. The inappropriate revisions would have destroyed my good name as an expert."

Keeping Privacy:

"I was researching for a book and I appealed to members of the public to write to me with their experiences. The result was about 25 letters but they mostly said the same thing - there was clearly not enough material in the subject for a book. I tried to sell the idea for an article to one of the sensationalist weekly magazines, and the features editor was very interested. However, he insisted on having real names and photographs.

As I'd promised total confidentiality to all who responded to my plea, I couldn't now ask them to participate in this.

The features editor pleaded with me, very sure it was a worthy subject. He even offered me a 'kill fee' (money paid even though the work was not eventually published). These were new heights in my writing experience so I said I'd see what I could do. I played around with ideas, and wrote the whole thing very convincingly, all about myself, but using a pen name. I duly sent the manuscript with a promise to be available for the photos they wanted, as I'm not photo-shy. It would be worth the money!

The article was rejected and I heard nothing. A month later I sent an invoice for the kill fee - asking for half the amount they would've paid for publication. This was all done by guesswork; I had no one to turn to for advice. The kill fee was paid within days, without question. I wished I'd put another nought on the end."

Sub-editor inserts mistakes:

"The girl phoned me and wanted to clarify some details of the recipes I'd sent in with an article. 'Should it be Self Raising Flour?' she said. We discussed a few ways of saying various things and her suggestions were all fine so I said go ahead and put those in. I thanked her for taking the trouble - because sometimes even I can't make head or tail of what I've written and she'd picked me up on it.

When the said publication appeared, the dear girl had inserted 'Self Raising Flower'. Luckily, the image of it made me laugh. I wondered what the readers thought!

I think a beginner would have been mortified. It takes confidence and determination to live down someone else's mistake."

It's easy to get an inferiority complex:

"The reader had clearly been doing something else when he read my work and rejected it. He told me the title didn't fit the story. I don't think it was a case of obscurity in the story - he got the character's name wrong as well!"

"A Theatre Company cut great swathes from the script - I wished I'd agreed to go along to rehearsals, even though there was no money available for my expense."

"My TV film was selected for further development and by the time we'd all finished with it and made the thing, it wasn't much like the original idea. But I'd got a foot in the door. You do these things for progress: you have to."

"I had a TV Director interested in my screen play. He lived near enough for us to spend sessions together getting it right. There was a call for submissions that we were aiming for, and the TV company had already expressed interest in my little play. It all looked pretty hopeful. As a writer 'new to TV' they wanted me to choose and work with a director, and I felt lucky to find someone very keen and based near my home.

Every time he turned up he had a different idea to pursue, and we produced numerous draft versions to try to find the right one. Four months of sleepless nights and sixteen drafts later I discovered he'd never previously directed a drama. The submission date was only days away when he broke it to me (as if he'd never realised it himself) that all his previous experience was with documentaries.

The version we finally submitted got nowhere. My original idea was so contaminated I haven't touched it since."

You learn to know when you are 'nearly there'

"A good rejection is when you get a non-standard letter. Or better still, some hand-written (and constructive) notes on the title page. A bad rejection is when it comes back pristine clean as if unread, without even a compliment slip. Even worse, I suppose, was when my MS was returned covered in coffee stains, reeking with tobacco, very well thumbed but finally someone had scribbled 'Not for us'. This was after 8 months."

There are more rejections and you can share yours with other writers at: www.rejectionslips.com

Write from the Heart

If you're trying to write and get recognition, it isn't all doom and gloom. As a creative writer rather than jobbing journalist you will undoubtedly be writing, first and foremost, for your own satisfaction or sanity. There are plenty of reasons for writing (see Diaries; and Literary Clout) where money takes the back seat.

Write what you want to write! There are ways of finding your niche. All you have to do is research your markets well, hit it off with someone high up the ladder, or - resign to that old cliché - sleep with editor. Remember, clichés are such because they're well used and common.

The View from 'Up There'

An editor writes:

> "Yes I've got my favourite writers, people I can rely on. There's one in particular who I know I can call on in emergencies. She'll produce something relevant, the right length, right style - you name it.
>
> Yes the ideal is to receive unsolicited copy ready to be planted straight into the column, something that really fits the bill. A piece of writing which takes the readership forward in the direction our magazine wants to go - but this kind of thing is like gold dust.
>
> We all want to be able to write great work, and unfortunately those who have the freshness to do it, just can't tailor their writing to the style and length and everything we have to produce."

Another editor says:

"Everywhere you look in the How To... books and mags, writers are told to send hard copy in double spacing, wide margins, pages numbered - but do they do it? You wouldn't believe the number of MSS I receive that totally ignore the 'conventions!

No numbers on the pages, no names, no covering letter, no SAE. We've started putting SSAE because people don't put the stamp on!

I can't cope with phone calls from hopefuls - well - I have to be in a thoroughly happy mood if I do. People expect me to know what they're talking about without my having the copy in front of me. Well it might be, of course, but which one - in a pile a foot deep? Oh if it were so memorable that I could find it and fall-in with their conversation straight away!"

And another:

"If I sense a professional, reliable approach to life, and potential for more of the same quality, then that writer stands a chance with me. I've got a job to do, a readership to satisfy, and a boss who demands the best - which is why he chose me. Writers I can't rely on or who are so damn snooty about their precious work - they fall by the wayside very quickly indeed."

Agents have the same problems

Carole Blake, Literary Agent and partner in Blake Friedmann Agency says in her book 'From Pitch to Publication',

"Publishers and agents are not welfare organisations: they cannot offer detailed editorial criticism for books they will not publish or represent."

Editor of a voluntary group magazine says:

"I have one chap who writes local history that's very relevant to our publication. He is terrifically succinct and very good at making bare facts sound as interesting as a good gossip. He doesn't type or even write legibly in longhand, and his work arrives on torn-out reporter-pad pages. It's very hard to read all capitals scrawled in soft pencil, but you know, his offerings are worth all the work they entail. Certainly for me, publishing this local magazine. And to see his face when it's all printed within the book - I almost relish his next idea."

It's Up to You

To repeat from our notes on your mission statement; how far will you compromise? How serious are you in pursuing that particular publication? Learn to answer these questions for yourself. Find your own direction.

Section Two

Liberation!

When you express yourself through words on the page or screen, you can discover a refreshing feeling of freedom. This chapter, and further chapters in this section, will show you how to open doors and windows in your mind that you never knew were there.

If you sit in your usual surroundings to write and find that it results in no writing at all, then you need some of this Liberation! Are you so bored with your own thoughts that you wonder why you bother to try and write at all? You need fresh air! You need some mental stimulation.

Maybe you're feeling strangled by the mundanity of your life or simply uninspired. Writing can set you free, but then you know that already. You only need to rediscover it.

If you're bored with your 'voice' and need to find another, the chapter on style exercises may help. If a piece of work is giving you pain from which you cannot get away; one of the style ideas could change your mood. Even if you decide not to use a new style, you might feel better about your writing after trying some different voices. Alternatively, making a change to a different style could give you the confidence you lacked.

Perhaps it's the very act of writing that you need to get away from? If you don't want to wash dishes (water is very therapeutic) then turn to the Creative Frolics chapter. These ideas will get you out of yourself, out of your rut and away from your fed up mindset. They'll help you start thinking visually and you'll feel so refreshed.

Are you feeling bogged down with the politics and shenanigans of the publishing world? You're not alone because everyone feels like that sometimes. There are some stories worth reading in Grouching Therapy, so make sure you dip-in to read how others can look back on their experience. If you can share some of your own, write to either bernie@author.co.uk or trevor@author.co.uk.

Be Bold, Be Different

Perhaps it's only contempt for the familiar that's tying you down. Here are some simple ways to snap out of it :-

Travel to another town

Preferably by public transport so you can observe the other travellers - and sit in a café to write. Park your car in an unlikely location, even if only in a different part of your usual car park, and sit and write, in the vehicle.

Go Back to Nature

If you have a story or project to pursue, that you really do want to get on with, then heap all your reference material into a rucksack, along with a hot flask, sandwiches and a groundsheet; and go somewhere you have never been to before. Find a tree and a seat or a patch of grass if you can (both for the oxygen and to atone with nature) but do especially get away from the interruptions. Leave the mobile phone at home, make a break from your email addiction, and avoid eye contact with any passers-by. It is surprising how much you can write when you're deeply focused.

Wear a blindfold to test your senses

Next time you eat a meal (not straight from the oven or microwave, please), cover your eyes and eat slowly; feel the textures with your tongue, taste the differences. After the meal, remove your blindfold and write down the descriptive words for the tastes and textures.

Stay blindfolded

It could become really exciting to play feely games with food and other materials. Have your partner place items in small dishes in front of you, then you feel each one in turn. Try, for example:

    Pickles
    Beetroot
    Raw egg and yolk
    Soil from outside
    Cold porridge
    A few dry cornflakes
    Dried fruit
    Vegetable peelings
    Root ginger
    Soft fruit of the season
    Twigs fallen from the tree

Now get your partner to tape record or write what you say these items feel like. Use the words to extend your vocabulary, and write a story with the ideas.

Write more by hand

Believe that you can write just as well - if not better - by hand than on a computer, in the first instance. Even if transcription is essential before anyone else can read it, the act of writing by hand will set you free to write from the heart. Sometimes the PC is your worst enemy. Go get some oxygen. Hug a tree!

Keep Trying

You may not know that emotional hang-ups are your problem. The Therapy chapter will give you some ideas, and help you turn problems to progress. You could emerge with a new project, sweeping old feelings into the past.

People often say they need someone to write for, to feel it is worth writing at all. Perhaps you need a tutor or mentor to give you personal encouragement. "I feel I can write anything for you," says one of my Writing Life students.

We discuss some aspects of the creative process - putting thoughts into words - in the chapter entitled Creative. As an adult you have imposed numerous inhibitions upon yourself for the sake of dignity and responsibility. In doing so, you may have quashed the fresh spontaneity of childhood. Go to Creative Frolics and rediscover that feeling of freedom.

Whatever works for you: do it! Liberate yourself, because your writing ambition deserves it.

Get a Life!

Take a life - any life . . . . .

Routines give us security. Patterns make the days bearable but they are also the basis for boredom, and many of us get stuck in a rut we don't really want. Gossip - oh yes! A scandal or an accident - we're ashamed to admit - helps the time pass more quickly.

A rumour in the office gets everyone excited. Partners at home will then say "What's got into you?" making you realise - nothing much at all, just a new view on something you've been looking at for years. And yet it was enough to change your mood, create conversation where silence once reigned. Something so small has put a smile on your face, perhaps instigated a decision, lightened up your day.

"Life? Don't talk to me about life. I haven't got one," said Marvin the paranoid android in The Hitch Hikers' Guide to the Galaxy by Douglas Adams. In a dull job, we can feel that way too.

Change the Way you Think

You might think your life isn't worth writing about, but the simple gossip that perked up your spirits for half a day proves it's not what you do but how you think about what you do that makes the difference.

Writing is a tool of thought. You can think and imagine on paper, on screen. You can write the scenarios of humdrum happenings and it will make you look at them from another point of view.

Every story has a blind spot. The gossip in the office is usually triggered by a revelation of something to which everyone had previously been blind. Every person has a blind spot. There is at least one thing, probably several things that we don't know about ourselves. These blind spots in life are what make fiction and biography so fascinating.

Our blind spots lead us to eavesdrop on conversations that might throw light on who we really are, who we are thought to be.

"I heard the boss say we're all on the list for redundancy," might not be what you want to hear.

"But you're not," makes you wonder what else was said? Could it be because of. . . . . .?

The blind spot is the interesting part. It's where your imagination fills the gaps. Always look for it, as it's sure to be there. The less you know, the more you imagine.

Stir the Ingredients

Novels grow from the writer's desire to explore a character and the way he or she develops, or achieves a certain goal. Not so simple when - to be believable - the blind spots have to be there and invisible for the reader. Add to this a certain amount of leverage exerted by the author through actions, events, and the other characters' agendas. Writing a novel sounds harder than coping with life itself, especially if you're the sort to just let life come at you.

Writing a biography or autobiography is different because there are often truths that need to be exposed and examined in some detail. Truth is frequently less believable than fiction, not least because timing and bureaucracy come into play. To be true to the facts you must write persuasively, explaining the unlikely sounding events until the orchestration makes sense.

Sensational stories are golden material to writers and I've heard seasoned writers like Jilly Cooper say we should all read the tabloid press in order to liven up our work. Nobody knows what goes on behind closed doors and good novels can reveal some of these hidden secrets. In the novel there is ample space for depth to explore the psychological nuances of life.

Look for the Depth

A good biography will explore the mind of the subject rather than seek information about private affairs. Unless you have a lot in common with the subject, reading the biography of a person can be rather uninteresting. A book must offer more than a catalogue of public achievements and so it seems usual to 'dig out the dirt' as is often the wont of the tabloid press.

Making friends with your subject and learning to understand them will surely reveal what makes them interesting in the eyes of your readers. A fine example of a biography that does just this is 'Inside the Mind of Gene Roddenberry' by Yvonne Fern.

Sensationalism soon becomes boring and vulgar. Stanley Spencer and Enid Blyton can be described as two harmless, well-known figures of the 20th Century - or were they?

If you read their biographies you might change your mind, because their ways of life were less than attractive. Both were prolific and passionate about their work, which is why they became so great. These are some of the strengths biographers should be exploring.

Real lives are useful starting points in weaving stories, creating sagas, exploring historical events in a fictional way. Biographies and obituaries can get you thinking.

Find New Ways Into a Character

There does exist a darker side to all characters but why, as writers, should we become ensconced in misery, deprivation, or deviation for the sake of a strong story? There is no need because even dull events can inspire new viewpoints that explore the disregarded subtleties.

How can we do that? The psychologist Albert Ellis developed an understanding of human behaviour in which he proposed that an experience triggers a thought; a thought triggers a feeling; and we then behave according to our feelings.

When behaviour goes wrong, for example: beating of a partner or spouse, child-abuse, illicit sexual relations, or other sensational actions, it is because that chain reaction of thought, feeling, action, has become distorted from acceptable morals.

See the Patterns

Experience > Thought > Feeling > Behaviour

The distortion is usually an overreaction centred on the feeling that stemmed from the thought.

'He tried to push me in the ditch!' creates a feeling of revenge and . . .

Wait! Before you push him in the ditch in revenge you must think 'Was it deliberate?' The rational person with high self-esteem will reconsider. 'No, he simply misjudged his footing.' Revenge will be quelled; the feeling will turn to something less lethal.

Experience > Thought > Feeling > Behaviour

. . .ditch? > pushed?> Revenge? > .."You take that!"

Change the Pattern

Or, with a moment's reflection the same situation could result in:

ditch? > slipped? > unsteady? > "You okay?"

True lives are a reliable source of inspiration for writers of fiction. I was recently hooked on the idea that Florence Nightingale wasn't everything she's remembered for, and thought it might make a subject for a play. Ten years from today, when I've been inspired to write a few scenes as drafts, the way to turn it into a plot might come together in my head. Then maybe the idea will be ripe to develop into a full play. You have to be patient and give ideas time to bear fruit.

In a random browse through the Dictionary of Biography

I stopped at Queen Mary I - daughter of Henry VIII. Questions sprang into my mind as I read that she was the sole survivor of six children. Without doing too much research (thereby excluding certain possibilities and restricting the imagination) here was the framework of great drama.

Remember: experience - thought - feeling - action.

Questions that might produce interesting results if they were answered:

> As each new child was born, was she aware of its death?
>
> What was it like to have Henry VIII as her father?
>
> At 34 she married Phillip II of Spain - how did they meet?

How do you imagine she got the nickname Bloody Mary? There is an historically verified answer to this question but it needn't stop you exploring the possibilities of rumours that might have prevailed at the time.

Ask Questions

One life history, many possibilities, and if you make it clear to any protesting 'experts' that you're fictionalising the story, there's nobody to say you are wrong. Of course there are historically verified answers to questions, but you can weave anything you like into fiction. Every life has so many avenues to explore; you need never be stuck for a subject.

Do steer clear of living icons, always present the work as a fictional dramatisation, and watch out for infringing copyright or libel boundaries!

Nothing so Famous?

True stories that belong to other people are often the easiest to embroider into fiction. They are certainly easier to fictionalise than your own. The mundane nature of any event means the piece can be challenging to write in an interesting way. Anoraks' walking dogs, ladies at knitting circles and grey-haired pensioners' outings are pretty clichéd subjects; but written from a new angle, a well-trodden subject will find new life and could even be surprisingly cutting edge. Take a look at the chapter on Experimental Writing, or Write with Style, as either could provide fuel for a new angle on a dull subject.

Inspiration to Draw Upon

Here are some problem page letters to get you thinking about how you might be able to throw light on them through fiction.

> 'Dear Auntie,
> I love my job and find it very challenging. My husband has always been a taciturn chap. He's a professional and loves his work too, though it's steady and it suits him. I love gardening and having hobbies of my own, so it's not as if I'm a leech or a nuisance chatterbox. The trouble is he never enthuses or encourages me when I have some good news. Last week I came to realise the extent of the problem when I won a contract for a very prestigious job. I rushed home to tell him but instead of congratulating me and discussing how I'd tackle the task, he only grunted something like, "Huh! Good for you!" Then he stuck his head in a book and seemed annoyed if I tried to get him talking. I've realised it's futile the way our marriage is going down hill. I feel more alive when I'm alone with my own thoughts rather than trying

to get blood out of a stone. Soon I'll be too
lonely and depressed to do anything about it.
~ Shirley. '

Auntie will not reply to Shirley because this scenario is the perfect pathway to a fiction - perhaps a novel. You can see one interpretation further on in this chapter where the taciturn husband gives his account. The problem isn't solved - it merely opens out possibilities. If they could separate, would they be happier? Would the husband still be disinterested, would Shirley still expect him to enthuse? What are the patterns of behaviour that have led to this situation? Look for patterns, invent patterns! It takes two to ruin a marriage - doesn't it?

Decide on your viewpoint for the narrative, and what the voice will be able to say (remember there are blind spots, for each character, in a story). Visualise an incident at home with Shirley and her taciturn man. The natural way might be to go with Shirley's viewpoint as it's presented as her problem. However, try writing the scenario from the husband's viewpoint. He might not see a problem and he has goals of his own but is aware that Shirley clearly wants something different.

Adapt your 'Voice'

Further ideas about voice and viewpoint can be found in Writing with Style, and Experimental Writing and Therapy. An adventurous way to tackle a story is to write in second-person-poetic:

> You come home
> Blethering.
> Some new contract
> And you don't give a damn
> About my day, my feelings.
> You turn off the radio
> Just when I want to hear

> And I watch you
> Watering the pot plants
> Without giving a thought
> To how it looks from here.
> Why should I fall at your feet
> In adoration
> Contracts fall through
> They always have before.
> Or they worry you
> And make you
> A misery to live with.
> Shirley be grateful
> For the happiness
> You bemoan.

There's a lot of fictional fun and understanding to be gleaned from writing stories based upon genuine problems. Many marital scars are caused by one partner's habit of mind-reading the other's and - by the nature of one being less communicative than the other - imagination plays a big part. ("He hasn't spoken therefore he disapproves, and so we won't ever be happy again!")

Don't Make Assumptions

Inaccurate mind-reading coupled with evidence from previous experience doesn't make a good novel. It would create one that's passive and introspective to read. There needs to be action, interaction and evidence of behavioural change. We are back to Ellis's sequence of Experience > Thought > Feeling > Behaviour and the characters' various blind spots adding to the intrigue.

There comes a time when you can't learn about it or theorise about the mechanics of writing, any longer. You simply have to get on and write it. So here are some more Agony Aunt letters to play around with.

'Dear Auntie,

Sam and I lived together for nearly ten years but when the relationship became very stale I could stand it no longer. I'd got things I wanted to do with my life and there's still time for me to have a baby. I was pondering for months on how to bring about a change (our sex life was always a bit disastrous - he's got a nervous skin condition that would often make it painful to be touched) when one day he suddenly said out of the blue, "I want to be a hermit." I was taken aback but in a way it was my answer. To cut a long story short we do now live apart but I miss him terribly and I know he misses me. He's letting himself go and even though I helped him put together an ad for a housekeeper, he seems not to be interested. Last time I visited him I vowed not to go back, because he does his utmost to be distant and unaffectionate. It's as if the less I see of him, the less a bond we have. It upsets me to see him becoming so antisocial and peculiar. He could be a different person if we had children. Do you think I should insist we get back together or shall I never go back ever again? ~ Anita'

'Dear Auntie,
I don't know what to do about my neighbours. They make so much noise and they're making an awful mess of the garden. Trees are dying because their children swing on the branches and break them; and the parents light bonfires that scorch everything nearby. I really don't feel happy going in my garden and they're such abusive people I can't ask them to take more care. I want to move away but then why should my home life be ruined by other people's behaviour? I feel so alone and I don't know what to do because I'm frightened to stand up for my rights. ~ Lily'

'Dear Auntie,
My wife and I share a powerful bond in that when we met, nine years ago, I was recovering from drug addiction. She helped me through some terrible times and we're happily married with a lovely girl and boy. My work is important to me as it's the mental stimulation I always knew I needed, but it does keep me away from home more than I'd like. The trouble is, Kathy is bored or lonely or something, and seems to be eating to make up for whatever's missing from her life. When I come home I find empty packets and the money - well, it just disappears. She says it's the children and their big appetites, but she's getting very fat - too fat I think to be healthy. Last night I found her eating a cold pizza that was in the fridge from when I came home unexpectedly having had dinner with an important colleague. The kids were in bed and she thought I was in the shower. Somehow it all came to me then - something's not right. ~ Frank'

Remember the blind spots in every character's story, and consider the patterns of behaviour.

Your Life

There's no reason why you shouldn't try writing your own life experiences, indeed we should all leave some record of our lives for future generations. Whatever way you go about it, there could come a time when it is published. You can make that happen. Even if you don't sail round the world, win an Olympic medal, save a life, or spend a year in prison, somebody, somewhere will be interested. As with every story, it's the way you tell it that makes it either good or forgettable.

For Yourself

In the first place, write it just for yourself. You'll be surprised at how much you know and have observed, because the world in which we live often is not revealed until you start writing. Include details like the weather that day, what was on the news, what were the prices for properties, a loaf of bread, a visit to the dentist, or a gallon of fuel. You can edit out the irrelevancies later, depending on your ultimate readership; and if this life story is to be for your descendants, please, leave in as much detail as possible. Historical accounts are so much more meaningful if the reality of daily expenditure is there to put the humdrum into context.

Only when someone reads your writing will you know whether you've captured the essence of what you wanted to say. Whether a memoir or fiction you need an informed opinion that can give constructive feedback. Don't ask an emotionally close person. Four critique services out of a large number that can be found include:

Writing Life specialise in helping writers to get started www.writinglife.org.uk

Hilary Johnson www.hilaryjohnson.demon.co.uk/;

Jacquie Bennett www.jbwb.com;

The Literary Consultancy www.literaryconsultancy.co.uk/

From the Heart

Include as much detail as you can. Often this is what separates the real writer from the ordinary person who does little more than write reports. Your observations make your experiences your own, and if you write 'from the heart' then your story - however mundane you may believe it to be - will be riveting for your reader. Despite the seriousness or businesslike manner of the exposition, writing from the heart will ensure artistic vigour seeps into the prose, making readers turn the pages until they reach the last word.

Experience to Fantasy

When writing fiction or drama, you want the work to be believable, and certainly not to seem contrived. How can you ensure this is the case? By putting yourself in the position of the character, writing from your heart, and injecting the 'imaginary' situation with real true-to-life observations.

Embrace the concept of Ellis's sequence:

Experience > Thought > Feeling > Behaviour.

Consider a sequence of events, such as: What if . . . this happened to her so she thought that, then she felt this, and behaved like - ?

Play around with the elements of the situation: feelings develop thoughts, and experience can create feelings! Back it up with sound characterisation through the way she talks (Talk & Tell) the way you tell it (Write with Style) and the extremes of her thoughts (Emotions, Arguments).

You may find it useful to look at the works of Sigmund Freud, Carl Rogers, and other psychologists who studied behaviour and tried to help individuals to get the best out of their lives. As a writer, that's what you're showing your characters trying to do.

Creative Frolics

Let Down Your Hair (metaphorically of course)

Here is a wealth of extraordinary exercises that might seem to have no connection with writing, but when you've played with any of them, you'll be refreshed and maybe write a best seller.

~ Take a Breath of Fresh Air ~

Kick your feet high and let your mind go with them.

Clap your hands above your head - now don't cringe.

It's Writers' Playtime! You need to get out of yourself.

You need to be silly, or become as expressive and uninhibited as a child.

Strictly for grown-ups -

As these guidelines are too easy for children. Find time for;

No word games.

No reading.

No writing.

The idea is to excavate the mind in order to liberate your pure - if naturally unclean - self.

Find your unencumbered and unpolluted mind: the creature that lives privately inside.

For a Week - DO NOT:

Read books - a newborn child cannot read.

Read newspapers - the natural child is blissfully ignorant of opinions.

Read children's books - they influence your writing style.

IF YOU MUST:

Read road signs - they spark ideas. 'Beware leaping reindeer ' - 'Smile for the Speed Cameras'.

Look at picture books - your own narrative will undoubtedly be more interesting than the intended voice.

Devour copies of The Beano, Action Man and Marvel Comics - because you'll start thinking in images instead of thought-processes.

REGULARLY:

Take bubbles and plastic ducks into the bath with you - remind yourself what is mental relaxation.

Buy yourself some attractive bath toys and PLAY with them - miniature role-play will help your fiction writing.

Sit and lie on the floor and just watch the world going on - you know that 'knowing look' in a baby's eyes? You can know all that too.

Now - FIND:

Absorbent surfaces that change colour when they're wet - brick wall, old dustbin lid or paper.

Any old paintbrushes - wide and cheap bargains: not the clogged solid things you used last year.

A bucket - preferably clean without a hole.

Now - DO:

Pour water in the bucket. Use the brush to 'paint' shapes and patterns - and watch them dry.

BUY:

A tarpaulin/groundsheet - if you have no back garden.

Numerous cheap sheets of newsprint or sugar paper - the larger the better.

Powder paints in red, blue and yellow - large amounts if possible.

NOW:

Place the paper on the (protected if necessary) ground.

Mix the powder colours with water and a drop of washing-up liquid.

Smear it on the paper with whatever comes to hand - or with your bare feet.

STAND BACK, FEEL REFRESHED.

Experiment - with folding, screwing up, tearing, and looking.

Incorporate - other parts of your body - for different visual effects - if time allows.

Clean up - and wash down with gallons of warm water.

Don't you just love it?

Do these messy activities whenever you're stuck in a rut. Although they feel like a waste of time - especially as there is no end-product to look at (nor should there be) they will reward your writing.

If you feel elated during, or after, doing these exercises - or even thinking about doing them - then Writing Life® could be what you need. (The tutor can give you even more 'experiments' to take you into new realms of creative writing.)

More Fun

Like what you created? Go take a look at the work of Don Van Vliet; www.beefheart.com for rural abstract expressionist.

Now that you are free to write, go along to the Triggers or Therapy or Experimental chapters.

There is more to life than writing!

Vignettes

Those of us who live a writing life tend to write vignettes willy-nilly. Each one is a glimpse, a slice of life, a part of something that - given a character, some goings on, and something bringing it to a close - would make a believable story.

Vignettes are what we see or hear about and then want to describe. One day we might use them, but to write about them is to remember them and every memory makes a writer all the more rich with experience.

What do you do with them? Store them of course. Use them. Many TV ads are vignettes. The longer adverts might be mini story scripts. How many people say the ads are often better than the programmes?

Here's an example of a vignette 'After the Accident' I once submitted to an accident prevention charity. They ignored it. I knew it was a powerful piece and was determined to make good use of it. After a few months I turned it round from a sad horrifying image to a love story.

'First Errand' was another vignette, inspired by the sight of a child playing on the floor and hearing an argument that made him ask for his favourite pudding.

When you live with your writing, each piece - however small - will find its rightful place.

After the Accident - a vignette

Irena lay on the hard, high, hospital bed, unmoving. Her eyes remained closed or barely open, tears ran down her temples now and then. She'd wipe them away with a bandaged wrist. She couldn't turn to bury her face in the pillow. Her mourning was stilted, like her hips and legs - restricted in a plaster cast.

"We've brought her to see you," said the sister.
too far down. She painfully lifted her arm over the

sleek, black hair; caressed the shoulder with three weak unbandaged fingers and settled for stroking her daughter's little face. It was a concession to the warm embrace she yearned.

After the Accident. This version © Bernie Ross 2001

First Errand - a Vignette

Jonathan was piecing together the chimney of his Lego factory, when he heard his name mentioned. Mum and Dad were talking in the kitchen.

"But you don't know what it's like," she was saying. "School holidays are too long. Specially in summer. When have you ever had to stay at home, day after day, week after week...."

"Chance would be a fine thing!"

As they talked, Mum's voice was weaving between raised tones and whispers. The tap was being intermittently turned on, drowning the conversation but revealing a few odd words.

"Envious."

"Can't go anywhere without money."

"Has to be taken out sometimes."

"You don't know..." Mum's voice was indignant.

"Haven't any money?"

"For God's sake woman."

"When I was eight years old..."

"Fishing"

"Climbing trees."

"Can't keep him tied to you for ever." Dad was angry.

The Lego chimney wouldn't go together right, two pieces fell off. Deep in concentration Jonathan picked his nose and wiped it on the carpet. Then he tried the pieces again. More arguments drifted in to his hearing.

"Strangers..... Not safe on his own."

"Independence..... get yourself a job.... Grown up soon..."

"You never know who he might..... "

"Strangers."

"Children abducted"

"But it's...."

A lorry slowed outside the front window, its great walls juddering, exhaust pipe shaking.

"Have to go anyway."

Giant wheels grinding - "You always leave it half discussed, we never..." - tyres slowly and clumsily squashing out of shape over the concrete kerb stones at the front of the house, their hot rubber smell catching in Jonathan's breath.

Dad came into the living room, he had his boots on already. They were the boots he wore when he went away for a long time, driving a long, long long way and not coming home for days and nights.

"Off now then, Jon," said Daddy. "Be good for Mummy."

A prickly kiss. A whiff of corned beef sandwiches in plastic. Two more bricks needed to go on the chimney.

Two men, one of them Daddy, talking outside. The lorry pulled away. Mum was drying her hands and the kitchen was quiet.

"I wish I could go with Daddy."

Mum switched the telly on and slumped into an armchair.

Later that day, Jonathan ran down the road in his sandals. Be careful down the hill with the big road at the bottom. Don't drop the money, you won't forget what to get will you? It wasn't quite time to start flexing his muscles for braking to a slow trot. It felt funny not to have Mum there behind him, telling him to slow down, he was so used to her voice that it was as ordinary as his own thoughts. Not quite time yet for using his leg muscles as brakes to stop running at the bottom of the hill, where cars and lorries thundered past and cyclists increased their pedalling to build up speed for climbing the next hill.

He tried to remember the shopping list his mother had recited to him: 3 slices of ham, 2 pounds of carrots, and a packet of Instant Whip. Or was it 2 slices of ham and 3 pounds of carrots? He knew it was only one packet of Instant Whip though. Jonathan's favourite. Just imagine 3 packets! I can't believe anyone but the Queen could be rich enough to have 3! Why isn't she fat? I bet she's got a room full of Instant Whip packets at her palace!

It was a real treat to have a bowl of Instant Whip! Pink and creamy, the feel of the spoon sliding into it and sucking up a huge dollop. Jonathan felt his dry mouth moisten at the thought. He would drop the big spoonful back into the bowl because putting such an enormous helping into his mouth, in one go, meant it would be gone too soon.

No, he would slide the spoon across the top carefully, and eat each little bit slowly. Then he would scrape gently round the edge of the bowl, savouring every drop of the pudding, every creamy smear, every tasty morsel. He would slowly stroke the top again, and the sides, licking the spoon until eventually it was all gone.

Jonathan's tongue was just about to lap the last traces of pink pudding from the imaginary bowl when he arrived at the bottom of the hill still running. The momentum carried him into the road... screech....clatter... thump.... click click click click...... Oh it's only a bike ouhw my knees....

Jonathan landed on top of an old man, sandwiching him between the road and the bicycle. He scrambled back to his feet, one sandal loosely hanging by the strap round his ankle.

"Oh, ohoh... sorry," he said, catching his breath between involuntary squeals. At first he couldn't see a face. There was only a grey raincoat rising like a hump from the tarmac, then a wrinkly hand on the end of a long arm pulled at the frame of the bike. In a moment the figure and bike were disentangled. The white-haired man with brown scrunchy face, let out a heavy sigh.

"Yo' all right lad?"

"Yeh. Sorry. You hurt?"

Bending to his feet, the sandal leather was stiff to adjust.

"Nothin' that won't heal. Yo' need brakes on them legs o' yours. Lucky I wasn't a car, you'd have been dead."

"Goin' shopping, see."

Jonathan remembered the money in his pocket and smacked it, urgently. The bowl of pudding flashed back in his mind, it still had traces to lick.

"Go along then. Do as y' mum says and don't run down the hill."

How did he know Mum said that?

As he walked along toward the shop, Jonathan looked at the palms of his hands. Grazed and pitted with grit, they hurt badly now. The white-haired man cycled past and lifted his hand in reassurance.

Jonathan couldn't remember what to buy. Instant Whip, he couldn't go home with just Instant Whip. He turned and ran all the way back home, the money still jangling in his pocket.

At the top of the hill, where the lorry always parked outside his window, Mum was standing rubbing her arms, looking alarmed. Jonathan came to a halt and felt his knees sting as her skirt billowed out to meet him. He fell into her lonely arms. He was crying and shaking, and looking at his palms. He blurted over her anxious sounds, "I forgot what you wanted... and ....an' ....there was a man."

First Errand - Vignette © Bernie Ross 1994

Write with Style

Find your style and be fixed up for ever.

The Harry Potter phenomenon might persuade you to think that way, but if it were so simple (and it isn't) are you the kind of artist to be content thereafter? Hit the right spot and so gain a huge number of readers and the question of style might never darken your thoughts again. Can you find the style that reflects you and then stick with it? Oh! If only writing were so easy!

Natural Progression

Many people don't even start writing because they cannot find the right voice, tone or style for the things they want to say. Writing is a form of creating music, and reading is a similarly individualistic activity. Interpretation is all. Navel-gazing really won't do but it doesn't hurt to try new voices for each idea you want to write.

There are as many voices in the world as there are people, and never before has the English language been so accommodating. I invent words all the time and people seem to know what I mean. (If you are sick of the sound of your own voice, go to Liberation, Experimental or even Creative Frolics, to get you out of yourself.)

The worst thing about a style is when it's forced out of the writer; and the second worst thing is when the reader is confused or put off by the style. There are too many books in this world for anyone to struggle with reading something that jolts in their mind and makes them crave the easy voice they'd prefer to be reading.

Elegant Writing

Style is a word to associate with high quality, perfection and smooth diction. There is a tiny book that has been a bestseller for decades: it is 'The Elements of Style' by Strunk

& White. I wouldn't be without it and nor should any self-respecting writer or editor. It is American in origin but it will clear up any queries you have about 'correct English'. However, if you adhere to every word in the book your writing will suffer; just as it will with adhering to any formal instructional book. 'Usage & Abusage' by Eric Partridge and the 'Cassell Guide to Common Errors in English' by Harry Blamires, are another two useful reference books; but please - trust your instincts to write an easy flow, and check on correctness later. This is especially important in creating fiction.

Showing

Don't you just get fed up with reading or hearing instructions to 'show - don't tell'? Journalism requires reportage, and reportage requires telling, so you can do that easily, as long as you know the facts. 'A single person moved into a house' - is a fact. However, it isn't effective fiction-writing.

'From what I could see there was only one person moving in to the house.' This is telling, and it's telling us just as much about the narrator as about the person moving in.

'Two strong men dressed in overalls shifted a sofa out of the van. The taller, older chap spoke to a woman who nodded and led the way up the path, took a key from her pocket, and opened the door. She stood back as they manoeuvred the sofa through the entrance.' That's showing.

Yes it's longer but it paints a picture of the individuality of the house-move itself. The reader's mind and further descriptions will fill the spaces and we could use the whole episode - with more detail of furnishings delivered - as a character sketch of the new neighbour. (Loads of pot plants? Regency style furniture? Ikea shelving?)

Embellish the Picture

Students have said to me they can't envisage writing anything long enough to be a novel. I soon show them what a difference can be made to the whole mood, picture, and atmosphere of their stories if only they adopt the 'showing' style. By showing what goes on, you make the reader active in interpreting the story. The joy of reading is in the realisation of a sequence of events that result in a question or a truth becoming resolved.

We look at what constitutes a story in the 'Plots' section. Find your showing style and you'll become intrigued by the potential twists and turns that appear in your own fiction. With sufficient depth of character and unfolding conflicts, your novel will be long enough.

Style Exercises

Perhaps there is a piece in your writing that really isn't working, or maybe you simply can't find the right voice for the paragraph that is pivotal to the story and highly important as a hook for your reader. What do you do - let the whole idea die on you? Within the following exercises you may find a way of rewriting that part.

Okay so I'm gonna suggest some new styles of writing that might just hit you where it matters, and help you write that story that's been bugging you for yonks. By the way, switch off your spell-check for these style games, and be free to invent a voice.

Style = Tone = Voice = the Music

Discover 'musical' styles. Consider, too, the music that would play in the background as you create each of these voices.

Observe a building near you

Think of its history, what it was originally made of, and what it looks like now.

a) Write about the building in the voice of a uniformed guide who escorts visitors in their coach-loads. It is an excursion for them to remember, but to you (the guide) it is run-of-the-mill.

b) Describe the building as if you're a pigeon. You're partly responsible for the white patches down the external walls but you like it that way.

c) Write about your day as the janitor. You are grouchy and lazy, complaining of overwork, so explain what work.

d) Pretend you built that place: it's your pride and joy. Describe it in beautiful prose, the sun shines out of its foundations.

e) Burglars are breaking in. Try writing the story as one of the thieves, determined to snatch the single object of value.

f) Describe the building as if it were for sale in an estate agent's window.

g) The building is destined for demolition, and you are the engineer putting in a bid for the job to destroy it. Describe how you would achieve the demolition, with the most advantageous outcomes.

Every one of these 'voices' will have a different 'style'.

A new tack: pretend the building is a wooden garden shed.

a) Try any or all of the ideas for writing as the tour guide, the pigeon, the janitor, the architect, burglar, estate agent, or demolition expert.

b) Become God. The omniscient being, seeing and knowing all things: getting inside everyone's head as they visit the shed and start to interact with each other.
c) Become the shed. How does it look and feel to be such a centre of attention? Describe all who pass the threshold.

Stand at the door of the building or shed, and describe what you see around you.

Then try the same from:

a) the door of Buckingham Palace
b) the door of The White House
c) the door of Tutankhamen's Tomb

Style can leave you gasping or guessing.

Aim for Quality

"Unsaleability seems to be the hall-mark, in modern times, of quality in writing." ~ said Pearsall Smith, 1936. This was quoted in Cyril Connolly's famous book 'Enemies of Promise', and it remains a classic must-read because most of what he says in it is gob-smackingly true.

Quality is like beauty - it is in the eye of the beholder. Your own writing is the best because it is the truest for you (When you read a novel that warms you through and through, don't you feel in love with the author?). If the reader recognises that very special truth, it will hit melting point and touch the place in your reader's heart where it matters.

These are the moments where gasps of wonderment make all your efforts worthwhile. Be true to yourself and be remembered. If you write for the masses, you have to waterdown your words or simplify to 'telling' to make them palatable to all. You might live off the takings if you're lucky, but I know which alternative I prefer.

A simple vignette can change your mood

We're examining a very subjective area of work. See how this affects you:

> 'He took her down to the stony beach where the low sun cast long shadows. The dark patches trailed away from every rounded hump of pebble as if colour drained away when the sun couldn't reach. Beside her he clutched at her cold arm; together they zig-zagged, giggling, toward the ribbons of waves that washed the sand and left mustard foam bubbles to gently burst. "I used to collect different coloured sands," he said.
>
> "Stripy test-tubes you mean?"
>
> "I had a glass swan. Gave it a striped neck, but I had to top it up with builders' sand. So it had a yellow body. Shame that."
>
> She made a cooing noise and put one arm around his shoulder. The sand under foot was deep yellow, exactly like builders' sand. Their steps faltered out of rhythm and he broke free, laughing. When they started to chase each other, his sandals and her bare heels pounded the shiny surface and shot lumps of sandy droplets on to her tanned skin. The resulting mess clung to her legs, until her steps washed into the sea.
>
> "Darling," he shouted. "There are crabs around this part."
>
> "No!" she screamed and promptly tripped on a boulder. Down she went, face into the sea, hands grazing on the violent moving stones.

Laughing, he grabbed her, and pulled her free. He carried her to the dry pebbles and they lay down together giggling. "You liar!" she laughed. "Oh look, your trousers are drenched."

"They'll dry," he said, suddenly serious.

Suddenly quiet. Only the gentle folding of wave upon wave, from the wake of a thousand ships behind the horizon. Only the sound of her heart and the tingle of desire could identify that moment, with the sun in that position; that silence; that smell.

They stayed there, petting, until darkness fell.'

On the Beach by Bernie Ross, 1999

I gasp at the image of that seashore tryst, but I'm guessing at the connotations in the following little rhetoric;

> Me got five
> Me got ten
> Put them up
> In the tree
> Put them down
> Green and brown
> Suck 'em
> One by one.

Fingerlickin' by Bernie Ross, 2001

Voices

You only have to think of Arthur Conan Doyle's Sherlock Holmes' novels and you'll know what I mean about his unforgettable style.

- Try writing your novel in the style of one of the greats. Make sure it's one you like, and one that's good. Be aware of how the style influences you

- Try writing a synopsis for a book in the style of a nursery rhyme or

- Try writing your diary in the style of a Shakespearean speech

'Today my messenger thus spelled an early call. Fair morning hailed his presence with heavy hand. Clear waters circled to wet the depths, for measure uttered friend or foe? And as the wardrobe by some instinct shed; great swathes of clothing hither cast a graceful figure to avail the latch.'

(The postman was early today. The weather's hot and I was washing when he banged on the door. Luckily I had a dressing gown to put on so I looked half decent to go and open the door to him.)

- Try writing your last shopping trip in the style of a tragedy.

I searched the aisles, distraught and pleading to some higher power. "Where? Where can these things be?" Girls' faces whisked past in oblivion at my turmoil.

"Please - can you tell me where the custard is kept?" I asked a uniformed woman who has worked there for years.

"Not really, I'm afraid. I'm new on shift since they changed the layout."

Tears welled as I found a row of shelves displaying sugar . . . jellies . . . dried milk products . . . spices . . . But no custard. Nowhere to be found!

Gender Difference

- Try writing as the opposite gender.

They say women think aloud, and men have strong focus.

Deborah Tannen has studied the topic in great depth and one her best books is named 'You Just Don't Understand.'

There are numerous theories about gender differences, including the work of John Gray with 'Men are from Mars, Women are from Venus'.

Often when you're reading a very good fiction writer you cannot tell whether it's male or female, even if the narrative voice is in first person viewpoint. Try honing this skill so that your own gender fades to insignificance.

Master cross-gender writing, and learn to use a versatility to write in numerous voices; and then you can applaud yourself as having real style.

Triggers

'It's the writing that matters'

Once you start writing you'll be astounded at how much comes out in a short spurt, even if you didn't have an idea when you started out. It might just keep coming, and if so, don't stop. If it gets part way and dries up - well at least you have something to build on when your energy is renewed.

Build on It

As if you had entry to an ongoing or special event workshop, with author.co.uk you have personal friendly access to some very down-to-earth writing experiences. It feels good to know you're not alone, but it's nice to know you will be left to work in privacy, so the Triggers Area can offer you both. Try some of these triggers to get you going.

Activate a Cliché

As I open the Dictionary of Clichésat random it reveals 'Enemy at the Gate'.

Whose gate? Literally? Metaphorically?

Another random choice produces:- 'On Pleasure Bent'.

Write about either of these phrases. Clichés have developed in language through over-use, that's all. Find a new way of saying it, and your subject matter is instantly relevant to a majority - so it's potentially popular!

Adapt a Parable

Take a passage from the Bible, Koran, the Greek Legends or some other classic work and adapt it to a modern occurrence. Introduce TV soap characters to play the parts. Be there yourself if you want to. Focus on the meaning behind the parable, making a strong point.

Using 'Soap' characters - or indeed celebrities or politicians with changed names - removes the need to concentrate on character development when the parable itself is your challenge.

Treasure

Pick up something from a charity shop or boot sale. A pair of shoes; a buckle; a dented hip-flask; a kitchen tool. Describe the character that might have owned the object. Why was it given up for sale? Write the story. Then show it.

Newspaper Cuttings

The 'news in brief' section of a paper often yields some weird and wonderful starting points. Remember it's your story to bend and shape in whatever way suits you. The characters must be yours (not least to avoid libel) and their plights can be far removed from the tale you originally read. My story 'Dinner Time' which appears in 'Creative Writing the Organic Way' was triggered by a 'news in brief' cutting.

What Was Said?

Drop in on a conversation or make a note of an overheard phrase. In a café last week I heard "You wanna bit? Mmm, I'd love a bit o' that."

What if... this had not been a café but two mountaineers dreaming of the hot meal promised at the end of their trek?

"You didn't have to come with us, you could've stayed with Auntie Fazz..." as a father boarded a coach trip with three whinging children.

Listen out for phrases and use them to start an imagined dialogue.

Meeting the Famous

Start a sentence with 'Yesterday I met....'
  Wordsworth.
  Bill Clinton.
  Vincent Van Gogh.

Emily Pankhurst.
Queen Elizabeth 1.

Or get someone else to give you a name. Remember that using a celebrity is a short cut because the image is established in your readers' minds so you've no need to slow the pace with descriptions.

Keep writing and then finish with '.... we parted with a kiss.'

Listen Carefully

In Talk and Tell we discuss how to bring characters to life by giving them language. Even if you hear a tiny snippet of dialogue it's worth trying to write it as you heard it. Do the meanings change according to the facial expressions or body language? As a writer, you can exaggerate. Use artistic license to build something into a fiction.

Focus on Visual Images

The Visualise chapter will help you paint pictures with words, and create scenes as grand as in any feature film. It is often said that 'I prefer the pictures on radio' because images blossom from the words I hear.

Pictures or photos can trigger a great story. Look for natural situations where the subjects aren't posing for the camera. Cut out magazine photos and keep a collection to select from. This way you'll have a character, in a situation, a predominant colour and mood to trigger your imagination - and you're away.

Mould your Work to a Shape

The chapter called Plots will help you put shape and meaning into something that might otherwise remain a mere glimpse or Vignette. I remember that as a new writer I regularly started writing stories that I didn't know how to finish; and if Triggers has put you in that predicament then the rest of the book will help you turn everything you write to good use.

Keep Writing

By remaining focused on what you want for your writing, you'll be able to write any-old-thing and then decipher the quality input from the debris.

Eliminate time-wasting and write your way in to creating some unique works of poetic prose that will be valuable in years to come.

Talk and Tell

Motivate your characters with dialogue because it is their story, and they will tell it or show it.

Even if your characters don't actually speak, you must know how they would, know what is their lilt, and what would come out of the mind. Dialogue makes characters, even if the communication is silent body language.

"The essence of national identity is language," said Lord Roll, in a recent radio discussion. I would home in on that and say the essence of character is language. However, the word 'language' incorporates body language, clothing (an image statement above all others), and physical attitude. Without character there is no story, without language we cannot understand.

Invent Believable Characters

Every person on this world is unique. Every fictional character must reflect a unique quality. It's up to the writer to observe every nuance of human identity and use it to invent believable characters.

As young children can't decipher fantasy from reality, good fiction is so believable and shows such truth that we don't want to know it isn't true. Accurate dialogue makes a fiction utterly believable.

Filling in the Picture

Like many writers, I've found more satisfaction in writing plays than in writing straight dramatic narrative. I think this is because when the dialogue is good the audience can fill in the pictures and emotions in more effective a way than I could ever describe. (I'm also keen on directors and actors interpreting my work in their own ways so that it's always new.)

As a reader I want to get to the nub of interaction as early as possible so that I feel as if I'm there. A novel begins:

> "Surprised? I was dumbfounded!" Sheila turned to Mike, lifting her shoulders and eyebrows.
> "I didn't think you would be," said Mike.

From here, two questions cry out to be answered: What was so surprising? Wasn't Mike surprised at all? And from there on we're asking - why?

We invent the development of a person's thought process by almost joining in the dialogue ourselves. "I didn't think you would be," said Mike. Oh, no he didn't, I invented it because it was crying out to be said.

As I writer I see an advantage in revealing an idea in as tight and immediate a way as possible. Hooking the readers into dialogue gets them friendly with the characters, and - as in real life - the movements and the expressions indicate mood. If not, these are filled in by imagination or by actors on the stage.

The Reality of Interactive Dialogue

Though it takes some getting used to reading a play, with dialogue-only the reader is mentally filling in the pictures and determining what's in the characters' minds. This is much better than offering the omniscient viewpoint narrative; and the readers' interpretations are likely to be far more accurate. The omniscient voice sees and understands everything, like God; and none of us can do more than guesswork, which comes over in writing as confusing.

Here's a scene I wrote recently. The dialogue was praised for its lifelike manner. Perhaps your mind will fill in the pictures.

Excerpt from 'Strange Meeting' stage play by Bernie Ross

IN THE HOTEL ROOM. TERESA ENTERS, WITH A BANDAGED BROKEN ARM. SIMON - IN MOTORBIKE GEAR - ENTERS BEHIND HER, CARRYING A CRASH HELMET. HE THROWS IT ON THE BED, ANGRILY.

SIMON: What the hell were you doing up there anyway?

TERESA: Wanted to join you.

SIMON: Just being a nosey bitch, I know.

TERESA: I wanted to be with you. Share it.

SIMON: Well I don't see the point in that.

TERESA: Share the drama . . . You're always saying it's so dramatic, so powerful to be there.

SIMON: You made it a drama all right.

TERESA: I don't know why you're so nasty, I'm in pain you know.

SIMON: Well it's your own stupid fault. Coming up there and thinking you wouldn't be any trouble.

TERESA: But I wasn't any trouble. Until you started showing off -

SIMON: Teresa, you were in the wrong, you know that. You shouldn't have been there.

TERESA: Suppose you thought I'd go for a ride on that motorbike till you came back.

SIMON: Not likely! Trust you with my bike?

TERESA: What's it likely to cost, anyway?

SIMON: Half the price I paid for it new, probably.

TERESA: Oh God, this is throbbing.

SIMON: Well they told you it would. That's what the jab was for.

TERESA: No it wasn't. That was for tetanus.

SIMON: Well you've got pills as well.

TERESA: Yeh. Paracetamol & Codeine. Lot of good that's gonna do.

SIMON: At least you'll be all right in a week or two. Unlike my petrol tank.

TERESA: Oh that's right. Bike first, wife second.

SIMON: I told you. You shouldn't have been there.Cost me a fucking fortune to get that repaired, and I can't drive it. How will I get it back to Edinburgh, that's what I want to know?

TERESA: It's only a little hole and a big dent. Can't you bung it up with something?

SIMON: Huh! Vinegar and brown paper, I suppose. Typical!

TERESA: I was thinking of chewing gum, actually. Or that stuff like it.

SIMON: No I can't use bodyfiller, if that's what you mean.

TERESA: That stuff that's grey and smells like plastic.

SIMON: Yes I know. Used it on the Cortina. No I can't and anyway, where the hell am I going to find a body-repair kit round here?

TERESA: Oh God. Look I don't know.

SIMON: Fuck knows why you couldn't sit down by the Loch and read a book or something.

TERESA: I wanted to be with you! I came to find you! I've been stuck in this hotel waiting days and days .

SIMON: I told you it wasn't worth you being around till the weekend.

TERESA: But it's Friday, now. I arrived yesterday - I

said I would 'cos of the train fares. Anyway, why shouldn't I come and be with you?

SIMON: The whole idea was that I'd be on my own. Searching on my own.

TERESA: Oh God. Start that again.

SIMON: You don't seem to want to understand. I need to be alone.

TERESA: Yeh. When it suits. You shouldn't have left the damn thing there to fall over so easily. And you expect me to sort it out for you.

SIMON: Well it was your fault

TERESA: Oh God I'm not starting on that again. I can't think straight, I'm in agony. Look help me undo this. I'm going to bed .END OF SCENE

Notice how the speeches are short. The dialogue sounds natural because the characters express only one idea at a time. (The scene has been read aloud by a theatre group of experienced readers and it came over very well.)

For the purpose of the reading - and for publication here - I left out all but the essential stage directions, and I like to leave it to the actors (or to you, as text readers) to invent the facial expressions and body language.

If 'Strange Meeting' were a novel or short story I'd illustrate the non-verbal language with economic prose. There would be no need for detailed descriptions about Teresa's plastered arm or Simon's angry face, but I might describe the time of day by the way the light falls on the decor.

It's true that reality gives us people who talk a lot and who pile one idea on top of another in a speech; but spare a thought for readers and your audience - this is where artistic license is brought into play. Fiction makes more sense than reality.

Listen to real speech: a group of people talking about an event. The whole is greater than its parts because - if you tape record the conversation and play it back to yourself - you'll probably find that no single character makes much sense on its own.

If you find the style of exposition to suit your story, there are some extraordinary forms of dialogue and interaction to be explored without having to use a single quote mark! See if you can identify these literary deceptions.

Better still is dialogue without any descriptive tags. In the scene with Simon and Teresa you could tell who was talking by what they said. In the little sample at the beginning of this chapter, Sheila didn't have to say her words defiantly or anxiously or even loudly, but Mike began to bring out her real feelings through the dialogue that ensued.

Power Games

These go on all the time and at a very basic level they reflect the domestic interaction between;

> a parent to child,
> child to parent,
> adult to another adult,
> and an enormous number of combinations and variations on the formulae.

A manager to his assistant might have the tone of parent to child; but - as in life itself - the conundrums begin when the hierarchical expectations are overridden by personality and situation.

Jim is the boss, David is the counter clerk. They go for a drink and David is first to the bar.

> "You have to elbow your way in here at this time of day, it's so busy," says David, taking control.
>
> "Can you make that a bitter shandy? I can't drink the strong stuff at lunch time," says Jim.

"I'll stand in for you at the board meeting if you want," says David.

Then roles change:

"No you won't" says Jim. "You can't get round me like that. And I want you back at the counter by 2 o'clock, sharp."

Body Language

This includes personal proximity, facial expressions, involuntary movements, tone of voice, and gestures. An attitude can be interpreted by whether the character is open to suggestion - with hands behind head, chest pushed forward, legs sprawled - or closed in defeat, with arms folded, shoulders raised and head lowered, chest minimised, and legs crossed and tucked under.

> They go to sit at a table and David sees his ex-girlfriend. Instantly he pulls the chair away for Jim to sit facing into the room, so that his own back is turned to the woman. He tucks his legs under the table and leans forward to talk to Jim. The ex-girlfriend doesn't see him.

Signs and Symptoms

We are often unaware of how we read people's messages as they speak. There might be a hidden curriculum in a relationship that would be a challenge to unobtrusively write in to a fiction. Even if past behaviour is unknown to us as observers, there is no getting away from a variety of slants and interpretations that inadvertently tell us what to hear:

If a stranger walked over to you and said, "I don't know what to do. The Cash Point has just eaten my credit card," then your reaction would probably depend upon your reading the situation very quickly. If it were an elderly person looking pleadingly into your eyes then you'd probably go to the machine with them and see if another button needed to be pressed. If the stranger appeared to be shifty, unable to look you in the eye, or even looking at you with firm amusement in his or her eyes, then you might shrug it off with an excuse that you really must get away.

In every conversation there is a power balance. The clever dialogue-writer will be aware of who dominates at any particular time. It is only worth analysing when a piece of writing doesn't seem to ring true, because if you're conscious of these deep meanings whilst writing, it could curtail your natural flow and even spoil the spontaneous speeches that will make your fiction come alive.

Hearing with Inadvertent Slants

The most obvious, perhaps, is that when we find a person attractive, we tend to admire their ideas. We can't help it, we want to like them, and so we take kindly to anything they say - unless it's a totally repugnant idea. Inventing a conversation in a romance, therefore, is fairly easy - until the injection of conflict rears its ugly head.

Hence, if the novel isn't mapped out already the characters develop as the dialogue advances. I think this is good. For this reason I'm not a mapper and planner: when I'm writing a story or play I learn about the people and where we're all going (yes, me included) as I go along.

The reader's past experience of the character influences the interpretation of dialogue, by anticipation, and by prejudices held.

If something is said without an expected eye-contact, suspicion is immediately roused. My reaction would be 'this is a lie.' There may be judgement in the speaker's voice, or adverse thoughts; or false assumptions in the listener might distort the true meaning of the words.

Silent gestures can say far more than a doctor's admonishing voice . . .

" I really think you shouldn't be doing this. You're going to regret it."

Did he, would he, say that? Would he imply it but speak in a more neutral way?

Sometimes a simple question can be terribly weighted without stating the speaker's opinion.

"Are you sure you want to do this?"

- could be said with relish or with admonishment, recognisable only by the way the doctor's eyes move.

Relish = glint of precision as he inspects an instrument; Admonishment = semi-closed, darting eyes and no eye-contact whatsoever.

Things Aren't What they Seem

There are all sorts of impressions that can be wrongly construed in a conversation. They are the things we think about or worry about on the way home, and lying in bed later.

Being a fiction writer adds another layer of thoughts to the ones you already carry about in everyday life. One minute you're thinking about how worried your friend is over something you discussed, and the next minute you're thinking about what your main character would say if he met so and so. No wonder we writers are mad.

Untangling the knots of human relationships makes fiction-writing very interesting, and fixing their problems makes a satisfying story (see Plots).

Nuts and Bolts

Many people shy away from writing dialogue because they lack confidence in getting the grammatical marks correct. They get in a muddle about what is actually spoken, what's in the character's mind, and what's in their own mind.

The confusion over grammatical marks isn't helped by the different styles used in publications: single quotation marks; double quotation marks; or a simple hyphen; and it's even more confusing if characters' dialogue and titles are quoted in the same passage so that each needs differentiating. The only way round it is to follow the publisher you're aiming to please, or invent your own rule and stick to it.

Over to You

As with all these pages in the writing focus arena, there comes a time when you have to get on and do it, and keep doing it.

Get the Pen Moving - Talk, Tell, Show

Here are some starting points to help you get writing character sketches and become aware of the silent language they speak:

> Describe a person you have seen involved in an activity: a workman in the road; a bank teller; a butcher; colleagues at your workplace. Ensure this person is meeting and dealing with other people. Let us see the action and hear the sounds, but no dialogue - not just yet.

> Write about the appearance of the very last person you saw. Give him or her a fully physical description - clothes, posture, complexion, hair, length of legs, style of movement etc., but no voice and no thoughts.

> Take two character sketches and create a single personality who is trying to be successful. Define the success. Now visualise a group of individuals telling him what he is. Write their comments.

> Describe your (imagined) impressions on meeting a stuffy, formal, and very important person in an appointment. Say something daring or over-familiar to him or her. With what speech does he or she react?

Write down the words to a favourite Nursery Rhyme. (Jack & Jill; or Old Mother Hubbard; Humpty Dumpty or Sing a Song of Sixpence). Describe the scenery in which the 'story' takes place, and what the characters look like - as if you were the illustrator in an expensively created book. Now bring the characters to life with imagined dialogue. In Strange Meeting, this is how I got to know Simon and Teresa.

What If . . .

This is the time to start thinking "What if . . .?" and to begin examining the motivation of the character. Love, hatred, fear, anger, lust, survival, or greed - any of these extreme emotions could be the motivating force that gets your writing heading for its rightful destination. Get the characters expressing their thoughts. Put them to work. Have them say things for you.

Learn from play writing, because writing a story with a telling voice as if from a pedestal will only turn your readers away. Characters make stories and characters talk!

Some of our most eloquent statesmen have been playwrights. They have projected their ideas and comments about the world or politics through characters in their plays.

Bertolt Brecht 1896 - 1956 was a German Dramatist who aimed to express his Marxist ideas through theatre.

Vaclev Havel is the Czech playwright whose works criticising the communist regime were banned throughout Eastern Europe from 1968. However, with a new political wave, he was elected State President in 1989.

Irish dramatist George Bernard Shaw 1856 - 1950, aimed to make an impact on his audience's social conscience and their emotions. He wrote five unsuccessful novels before his first play was produced in 1892, from which, it seems, he found his niche.

It is no new discovery that Theatre and politics go together. Look at Shakespeare's comment on the governments of the time. Learning to write believable dialogue is a remarkably efficient way of making your mark on the world.

Visualise

Good prose creates pictures through words. You want your reader to visualise the picture you have in mind. There is a skill in this, and I hope to help you find it.

Like a Canvas

When I was an art student I had an idea to paint a violinist, but somehow I couldn't make it look the way I wanted it to look. I painted a board with matt black, and then painted the violinist, sitting on a chair, playing his instrument.

The 'different' thing about this painting was that the violinist was painted in black paint as well as his background: the violinist himself was in black gloss. The idea was that the gloss paint would reflect images and colours from the surroundings, whilst the viewer would look in depth at the figure and be able to see more details by moving toward it. They would also perceive slightly different images by looking at it from different angles.

Whilst at first sight the picture was a plain black board, I wanted to evoke the quiet and deep concentration of the violinist as he embraced his violin and all its potential. The viewer would only realise the true depth of the picture as he or she moved in closer. I wanted to call the painting 'Rhapsody in Black' and for it to fascinate the viewers with the effective use of paint; and help them to imagine the music that emanates from the instrument.

My problem was that I couldn't portray the lifelike image I wanted; and I could explain it all much better in words. This was when I realised I was destined to be a writer.

Observe, Think: Connect Detail

The key to being able to write vivid images lies in your ability to make sharp observations. These must trigger ongoing thoughts that make connections - both realistic and fantastic.

(You see a pair of shoes by the door and connect them with a visitor. If the shoes are muddy trainers the visitor is probably a teenage lad or a football-mad dad. Character, plot and story all begin to develop.)

The observations also bring *detail* into relevance. You understand why something is like it is, if you think about what you saw. Observation puts an image into perspective in writing - just as the right detail in a good painting or carefully focused photo puts an object into perspective.

(How important are those shoes you saw? Why does it matter they were muddy and the stones lodged in the mud were from . . .? [connect!] You show the details in the word-picture if they're relevant to what happens next.)

I have to say before writing more of this, that I find it extremely hard to define the process of visualisation. I feel I was born with it. It has been useful to analyse it though, and I think the description applies equally well to painting a picture on canvas.

Imagination

As a guide to my personal viewpoint, this is my definition of imagination:

> 'Imagination is the ability to take known facts (events, situations, or characters) out of context and put them into a new or expected situation. The result is a collection of (guessed) responses, some of which may be diverse, others perfectly credible.'

Can you write a definition of imagination that's accurate for how it is with you?

In 'Rhapsody in Black' I was superimposing the glossy image of the violinist on to his matt black surroundings. When I write a fiction I superimpose some of the close-up observations I've made during living, on to a background from another context, a different area of my experience. By doing so, I'm creating a new 'picture'.

We are all Creative in Different Ways

I was well into my forties before I realised that some writers think in an abstract, picture-less way. (One is inclined to think that self is 'normal' and everyone is like self.) I visualise *everything*, to the extent that each scene in a fiction or screenplay I'm writing has its own colour. Occasionally I will state it in the directions.

Since realising this phenomenon, I make all the more effort to give the pictures to my readers; since they might not visualise images as I think I do. So this is my challenge: to analyse the skill and pass it on to you.

There are some books about visualisation but I've not found them helpful in explaining this subject. They veer away from the ability to 'see an image in the mind's eye' and they teach you to use visualisation as a means to positive thinking: a healing method.

We writers are not looking for healing because we have our own methods. We manipulate ideas through rearranging words. There's more on this in the chapter on Writing Therapy. Like Kurt Vonnegut we, 'Treat our mental illness every day'. Reading is also a therapy: an escape. We can give our readers photographic images, or impressionist pictures, fantasy scenes and surreal atmospheres. We can transport our readers to new lands, give them new friends, show them new places and new experiences.

How? With adventurous visual descriptions.

Play with Images

One of the easiest ways to create a picture is to describe what something looked like. An uncommon sight can be compared to something we might see every day.

[So we get into defining similes and metaphors, but who

cares what it is you use? They could be quavers and crotchets for all it matters here.]

Write the description in the way that feels right for the prose.

Similes say things are similar -

e.g.: - as cold as ice; or, felt like an iceberg, or looked white as snow.

Clichés abound, but lateral thinking will come to the rescue.

Try these:

> His hands were as thin as . . . . .
>
> The sky was like . . . .
>
> Flower pots were stacked like . . . .
>
> Cars were queuing as if . . . . . .
>
> The clouds in the blue sky were . . .

Not so easy when you're faced with images out of their context? Tackle the *whole* image: If the man's hands were skinny then his clothes were probably bedraggled, his face long - and his hands were as thin as a clutch of dried twigs collected from his pristine lawn.

With the above exercises it might be helpful to close your eyes and imagine the whole picture, and write a description that helps to accentuate the character of the scene. Close your eyes and think of stacked flowerpots. Similes and metaphors will come to you more easily this way.

Metaphors compare an image or a fact *without actually saying so*:

'You've joined the club, then!' - euphemisms are metaphors too: 'The heavens opened on Tommy as he went to see a man about a dog.'

Or, more vividly: 'The stack of papers that were his divorce lay in the corner getting dog-eared and dusty.'

Try writing descriptive metaphors for these:

a broken marriage (Their marriage was a . . . .)

old age is . . .

a procession of people leaving work was a . . .

strobe lighting at a night club turned the place into . . .

apples falling in a garden were . . .

Metaphors and similes create strong, accurate images in the readers' minds. It's rewarding when you've written something and the reader says, "It's very visual, I felt as if I was walking there and could see all the same things." Another might say, "I know the place, I've been there, you even captured the smell."

Heavy Reading

Beware of bombarding the reader with too many images, however. A description of a walk around a Maritime Museum might accurately describe the atmosphere as the innards of a whale. However, if you start saying the seating was as comfortable as a cushion of fallen apple blossom; and the display cabinets were like microwave ovens emptied of warm bread and replaced with doll's house furniture, the reader will forget where you started. Add to this the litterbins were like his granny's; and the floor reminded you of the supermarket - then the readers have forgotten where they're meant to be. Long sentences throw them off your route, and they give up reading.

Some of the strongest writing can be found where a whole story is told via metaphor, where the lost love is compared to the stray dog, or the escaped convict is compared to a wild boar. The possibilities are endless and will always add a challenge to your writing as well as making for 'active' reading.

Yes - readers want their fiction to transport them into new

lands, or to show them new friends and new experiences. You are probably good at visualising, but perhaps you haven't yet found the confidence to paint your intangible pictures in words. The answer is to take yourself there and to then incorporate all the senses, not simply sight. Your observation skills will help you to write in an explicit way.

The word explicit merely means 'Precisely and clearly expressed, leaving nothing to implication.' This doesn't mean you have to explain everything, and render the reader totally passive. The sharper your observation and description of it, the greater the reader is able to judge the situation for himself.

Good writing that's vivid takes the reader there too. Come to this tea party with me :

Yoghurt - a sample of visual writing

> The chandelier has been polished this morning, like your shoes; and the walls display your relatives though no blood is shared, nor love.
>
> The large oval table has a starched white cloth camouflaged with shining silver cutlery. The plates are a delicate petal-painted china, translucent to the eye. We all sit with our hands neatly together, our lips pursed in tidy smiles as the hostess collects the finished dishes and accepts our compliments with exquisite grace. We wait, looking discreetly around at each other.
>
> I have seen you elsewhere in your posh clothes and with your charming smile, watching a young waiter deftly dishing food onto your plate with bright white-gold tongs. I have watched your unchanging expression as slices of inedible fat have slithered from the silver tureen onto the lustre-edged plate, to join the over-cooked roast potatoes and the rubbery sticks of carrot. And I

have heard you say, "Yes, lovely, thank you," as the smart man in his stiff white waistcoat asked, "Is everything all right?"

I am watching you as your face beams and your mouth waters and your eyes sparkle, as they follow your sister-in-law's ladle into the purple cream mixture and out on to your dainty dessert bowl.

"Mmm - home made?" you pronounce to all who sit politely round the altar of our focus of delight. "Your own blackberries too?" you say, as one especially dark piece of fruit falls into your dish along with several others.

I was watching when she washed the blackberries and picked them over. She popped them into the creamy yoghurt, stirring to create a delicate pastel shade.

I saw her proudly carry the pretty serving dish to the table, to the musical gasps of the genteel guests.

And I watch you now as you place the lilac coated bluebottle into your mouth. I see you cringe at the strangely bitter taste, and then swallow quickly to get back to the smile that you will inevitably insist is sincere.

© Bernie Ross 2001

Here's an exercise I have used in an evening class where businessmen have rushed off the train to arrive to learn creative writing and tired parents come to feed their heads with mental stimulation. I recommend you read this aloud into a tape recorder, pausing often; and play it back to yourself. Alternatively, get someone to read it to you. Try not to fall asleep.

The Magic Carpet

You are sitting on the floor with your eyes closed.

Between yourself and the hard floorboards is a deep red carpet with paisley patterns round the edges -

- and short tassels that are tangled but it doesn't matter.

 - Keep your eyes closed and relax as well as you can.

- The carpet is a little rucked up, you try to flatten it but there's strength there. It resists.

- Before you know it the carpet is rising, it has power of its own, with you on it! It is strong and comfortable, and you feel no vertigo at all.

- It rises and rises, and suddenly you enjoy it.

-You can feel the warm air at the top of the room and then -

- like magic - you are out in the sky.

- Keep your eyes closed, and look at what you see.

- Your home is far below, your town is small and smaller.

- The football pitch, the factory complex, the by-pass, the river, the woodland, the motorway . . . .

- Where are you going?

- Where do you want to go? Go then!

- Go. Go. You are flying on a magic carpet.

- Let it gently lower you down in a place you know and love.

- It is warm, and there are -

- Voices. Colours. Settle down with your eyes closed and take in all that you see in your mind's eye - in that place you imagine so well.

- Are you on the warm beach at the South of France?

- The calm seashore café under the stars?

- Lazing by the pool at a villa in Torrevieja?

- Are you resting in the hills of never-never land?

- are you drinking the excitement of a busy bazaar full of physical delights?

- What do you see?

- Listen, quiet.

- The sound of your own breath. The sounds all around you in your magical place are drowning the thoughts of who you are and convincing you that you're there, warm, relaxed, open to suggestion, to gifts, to all the influences upon your senses.

- Stay there. Consume the enjoyment with your whole body. Silent - seeing with your eyes closed.

- for a good five minutes ….

Okay we're coming back now. It's getting cooler.

- We are high in the atmosphere and our dreamland is out of sight.

- Keep coming.

- Keep coming.

- Don't fall down with a bump. Land gently, the carpet is still soft.

Open your eyes. Take your pen and describe.
Write about what you saw and what you felt.

Pretend you're Shakespeare in Wonderland or Wordsworth on an island, someone who wasn't you but it is you because you went there and you know what you saw.

Write non-stop for ten minutes. Make it 'automatic writing' - it needn't make sense, but the words will be those that help evoke that image, of that place, that moment when you wished you were really there.

'Cherry Tree' is a story that I'm told is full of pictures. I think it could be 'shown' better.

You can read the story at www.author.co.uk/cherry. What do you think?

Cherry Tree was inspired by the title and by a person who I happened to be sitting near when it was mentioned - someone who owned a large garden that was like a beautifully overgrown field.

A simple vignette will develop easily into something visual. First Errand is both a plain vignette and I've developed it into a short film script, at the request of a director who read it and saw the possibilities.

First Errand - A short film
by Bernie Ross

WE SEE A SMALL BOY CROUCHED ON A CARPET, HE IS SURROUNDED WITH COLOURED LEGO BRICKS AND IS ENGROSSED IN PLAYING WITH THEM.

THE ROOM IS COSY, UNTIDY, INEXPENSIVELY FURNISHED. THERE'S A DOOR IN THE BACKGROUND, FROM WHICH BRIGHT DAYLIGHT SHINES, AND EVIDENTLY LEADS TO THE KITCHEN WHERE SOME ALTERCATION IS TAKING PLACE.

ABOVE HIM IS A WINDOW SHOWING SKY.

WE SEE JONATHAN'S FACE AS HE CONCENTRATES ON PIECING THE BRICKS TOGETHER, AND WE

WATCH HIS CHUBBY HANDS AS THEY TRY TO MANIPULATE THE BRICKS AND GET THEM TO FIT.

HE IS BUILDING SOMETHING WITH A TALL CHIMNEY, BUT IT KEEPS FALLING OFF.

WE HEAR JONATHAN'S VOICE IN THE FOREGROUND AS WELL AS HIS PARENTS' ONGOING ARGUMENT - OF WHICH ONLY SNIPPETS ARE PROPERLY HEARD. (THE BULK OF THE DIALOGUE IS SET OUT AS A GUIDE FOR THE ACTORS.)

JONATHAN

Go on. Go on you. Chimney, you gotta go on there. For all the smoke.

HE STICKS HIS TONGUE TOWARD HIS NOSE IN CONCENTRATION, AND USES HIS CUFF TO WIPE HIS TOP LIP DRY. THE BACKGROUND VOICES ARE GARBLED SO THAT ONLY CERTAIN (UNDERLINED) WORDS LIKE HIS NAME ARE DISTINGUISHABLE

DAD

And what are you going to do with Jonathan? Take him with you -

MUM

Take him with me, of course, there's not much else I can do -

DAD

No place for a small boy, he needs to be outside, kicking a ball around . . . .

MUM

But you don't know what it's like, for goodness sake . . .

DAD

I know what it's like to be stuck in a job I don't like, in a factory doing the same old thing for someone else's pockets -

MUM

School holidays are too long. Specially in summer. When have you ever had to stay at home, day after day, week after week . . . .

DAD

Huh! Chance would be a fine thing! Think of the things I could get done around here -

DAD'S VOICE IS DROWNED OUT BY THE TAP RUNNING.

JONATHAN CONTINUES TO BUILD WITH HIS BRICKS.

THE TAP IS TURNED ON AND OFF, WITH CROCKERY AND CUTLERY SOUNDS.

THE VOICES CONTINUE, WHILST THE CAMERA FOCUSES ON JONATHAN'S PLAY. SOUND EDITING PUTS EMPHASIS ON THE EMOTIONAL RAISING AND LOWERING OF MUM'S VOICE.

JONATHAN'S ATTENTION MOVES MOMENTARILY TO DIFFERENT TOYS - ALL IMAGINATIVE SMALL-SCALE ITEMS.

DAD

I can't think why anyone should be envious. There's no glamour in it you know. It's tedious and mind-destroying, like most work.

MUM

But it's tedious and mind-destroying here all day can't you see that?

DAD

But you don't have to stay here, you've got the time to go out . . .

MUM

Oh yes? And where can we go? Where can I go, even, There's no-where. Can't go anywhere without money.

DAD

Course you can. Loads of places. Go to the park. Go and feed the ducks. Kick a ball around. Get the free bus out to the shopping centre . . . . .

MUM

Oh, and you think I don't do all of those?

DAD

I didn't say you didn't. But you make out you're chained to the house because of the boy. You don't need a minder. The boy needs to go out and get experience.

MUM

Well of course he does! He has to be taken out sometimes. And I like to go out sometimes too! But there's a limit. You don't know how much it takes in organisation and never having any money is hardly gonna give me confidence -

DAD

You don't need money, woman. Haven't any money? What sort of excuse is that?

MUM

You need money to go places. I can't take him out if there's no . . ...

DAD

For God's sake woman, and you think taking him to work with you will give you money and time to take him where he wants to go?

MUM

No but it will give us a bit more scope and he'll be just as happy with his lego where ever he is.

DAD

It's not healthy, if you ask me. Stuck in a shop canteen or

something while his mum works on the till. (HIS VOICE CHANGES FROM AUTHORITARIAN TO NOSTALGIC.) When I was eight years old I was keeping myself safe and busy -

MUM

That was different in them days.

DAD

Used to go fishing, with me little jam jar. Used to meet up with my mates down the track and we'd be climbing trees and . . . and fishing for tiddlers .. . . .

MUM

What when you were same age as Jonathan? I don't think so. Not that young.

DAD (FRUSTRATED)

I was I tell you. And that's what he needs. That's what you need. None of this business of palming him off to a minder to get a bit of space for yourself -

MUM

It's for all our sakes I was looking at doing it, and it's the best thing.

DAD

Let the boy find a bit of space for himself, is what I say. Or he'll be a nanny's boy all his life. YOU CAN'T KEEP HIM TIED TO YOU FOR EVER.

MUM

I don't intend to, either. But I can't risk - there are too many strangers . . . . . I can't let him play out on his own. Not safe on his own.

THE LEGO CHIMNEY WON'T GO TOGETHER RIGHT, SOME PIECES FALL OFF. DEEP IN CONCENTRATION JONATHAN PICKS HIS NOSE AND WIPES IT ON THE CARPET. HE TRIES THE PIECES AGAIN. MORE ARGUMENTS DRIFT IN TO HIS HEARING, MORE

CLEARLY NOW.
DAD
Sooner or later he's going to have to have some independence. When he's bigger you can get yourself a job
MUM
Well it could be now if only you'd let me take him. It's a creche. It's not going to be just him on his own . . . . . .
DAD
Well leave it. Let him have the summer holidays. Let him out to do some errands. He'll be grown up soon.
MUM
That's all very well you saying that, but you never know who he might get caught up with-
DAD (EMOTIONAL NOW)
He's too young for that. Too young to get caught up with the wrong sort.
MUM
No I don't mean that. You never know who he might . . . . .
DAD
Well none of us do, but you can help him learn a bit of responsibility . . .
MUM
Huh! You say that, but it's strangers. There are some weirdo's around, where ever you go. Local or not.
DAD
Well that's life isn't it. You can't mollycoddle him forever!
MUM
I don't know. Every day you hear of children abducted.

DAD

Yeh. And mostly it's by people they know. Divorce and what-not.

MUM

But it's so dangerous. . . .

FROM JONATHAN'S SITUATION WE SEE THE ROOM DARKENING AS A LORRY PULLS UP OUTSIDE THE WINDOW, BLOCKING OUT THE LIGHT. AS IF EXPERIENCING IT FROM JONATHAN'S SMALL STATURE WE SEE THE WALLS OF THE LORRY JUDDERING AND WE HEAR THE GREAT ENGINE LABOURING, THE EXHAUST PIPE SHAKING.

DAD

Well I have to go anyway. Derek's waiting for me now.

THE LORRY SEEMS TO BE MANOUVRING, ITS GREAT WHEELS GRINDING AND TYRES SQUELCHING OUT OF SHAPE OVER KERB STONES IN FRONT OF THE HOUSE. THERE IS BLACK RUBBER SMOKE.

JONATHAN SCREWS UP HIS NOSE, ACCENTUATING THE OPPRESSIVE, CLOSING-IN EFFECT THE LORRY IS CAUSING.

MUM

You always leave it half discussed, we never share a proper conversation about how best to -

DAD APPEARS IN THE DOORWAY AND APPROACHES JONATHAN. HIS BIG BOOTS DOMINATE HIS IMAGE AS HE BEGINS TO BEND DOWN TO HIS SON.

DAD (BRIGHTLY)

Off now then, Jon.

WE SEE DAD'S PRICKLY CHIN MEET THE DELICATE SKIN OF THE YOUNG BOY. MUM'S VOICE IS IN THE BACKGROUND.

MUM

You say this driving lark is better, but you're not even home to kiss the boy goodnight.

DAD

Be good for Mummy.

WE SEE DAD HOLDING A BAG OF SANDWICHES, IT IS A WoDGE ABOUT FIVE TIMES THE SIZE OF JONATHAN'S BRICK CONSTRUCTION ON THE FLOOR. THERE ARE TWO MORE BRICKS CLEARLY WAITING TO BE PUT ON TO COMPLETE THE CHIMNEY.

JONATHAN FOCUSES ON THE TASK. DAD AND MUM RETURN TO THE KITCHEN AND BACKGROUND .

MUM

I don't know how you can think this job is better than the factory. What do you think it's like for us?

DAD

You look after the boy. I'll be back before you know it.

MUM

He'll be grown up before you know it.

(THEN URGENTLY) Oh - You be careful now, give me a ring . . . .

A DISTANT DOOR CLOSES. MUM IS STILL IN THE KITCHEN, THE TAP RUNNING INTERMITTENTLY, SOUNDS OF HOUSEWORK, AS JONATHAN IS STILL CROUCHED ON THE FLOOR SORTING AND FIXING LEGO BRICKS TOGETHER.

OUTSIDE THE WINDOW, THERE ARE TWO MEN'S VOICES, INCLUDING DAD, SHOUTING ABOVE THE LORRY SOUND, BUT WE CAN'T HEAR THEIR WORDS. JONATHAN IS NOW SQUASHING HIS FACE ON THE WINDOW GLASS TO SEE AND HEAR MORE. THE MEN CLIMB UP TO THE CAB, THE JUDDERING

SOUNDS DOMINATE, AND THE LORRY PULLS AWAY LEAVING BRIGHTNESS TO RETURN TO THE ROOM. JONATHAN RETURNS TO HIS BRICKS. MUM IS APPROACHING FROM THE KITCHEN DOORWAY, SHE IS DRYING HER HANDS.

JONATHAN

I wish I could go with daddy.

WE SEE MUM'S REGRETFUL FACE WHICH INFERS 'SO DO I'.

SHE SWITCHES ON THE TV AND SLUMPS INTO AN ARMCHAIR. JONATHAN CLIMBS ON TO HER AND THEY REST TOGETHER. (JONATHAN WILL BE TOUCHING HER FACE OR HAIR AS AN INTIMATE CHILD DOES.) THEY GET LOST IN MUSIC-WITH-JABBER ON TV.

EXTERIOR

BIRD'S EYE VIEW:

JONATHAN IS RUNNING DOWN THE ROAD, AWAY FROM THE HOUSE.

MUM IS CLOSING THE DOOR.

NOW WE SEE AND HEAR THE WORLD AS IF INSIDE JONATHAN'S HEAD. (BACKED BY THE SOUND OF JONATHAN'S HEART BEAT, BREATH AND FOOTSTEPS, HE HEARS MUM'S VOICE:)

MUM

You want some Instant Whip for tea Jon?

MUM

Be careful down the hill with the big road at the bottom. (HIS FOOTSTEPS ON GRAVEL) Don't drop the money, you won't forget what to get, will you?

JONATHAN

Don't run too fast. (MONEY JANGLING.)

DAD

You need good brakes on that hill.

MUM

Slow down when you get near the bottom.

(JONATHAN'S HEART BEAT, BREATH AND FOOTSTEPS.)

BIRD'S EYE VIEW

JONATHAN LOOKS BEHIND HIM.

WE SEE HIS SANDALS HITTING THE ROAD AS HE RUNS, SO THAT HIS BARE LEGS AND FEET SEEM VULNERABLE. MONEY JANGLES IN HIS POCKET.

INSIDE HIS HEAD AGAIN:

MUM (MATTER-OF-FACT)

Slow down. Jonathan. Mind the traffic.

JONATHAN

Look mum, I can't stop, I can't stop!

MUM

Yes you can, silly. Slow down now.

THE SOUND OF OCCASIONAL TRAFFIC OVER-RIDES SOME OF THE THOUGHT-VOICES.

JONATHAN

I've got good brakes on my legs

MUM

You don't want to go head first into that traffic do you!

DAD

Watch out for bikes won't you!

MUM

They go faster so as to get up the hill easy.

DAD

You got good brakes on those legs

WE SEE JONATHAN'S FACE AS HIS THOUGHT

VOICE TURNS TO THE RECITAL OF HIS SHOPPING LIST:

JONATHAN

3 slices of ham, 2 pounds of carrots and a packet of Instant Whip

MUM

3 slices of ham, 2 pounds of carrots and a packet of Instant Whip

JONATHAN IS STILL RUNNING, WITH MONEY JANGLING IN HIS POCKET.

JONATHAN

2 slices of Ham and 3 carrots. No. Instant whip. 2 carrots and 3 pounds of ham

JONATHAN

3 Packets of instant whip!

INTERIOR

WE SEE AN APPETISING BOWL OF WHIPPED PINK PUDDING AND JONATHAN DIPPING HIS SPOON IN.

THE SOUND OF HIS RUNNING AND OUTDOOR ATMOSPHERICS PREDOMINATE AS WE SEE A CLOSE-UP OF JONATHAN'S FACE LICKING A SPOON AND GUIDING IT AROUND THE EDGE OF THE BOWL OF PUDDING.

THEN HE HAS A BIG BOWL IN FRONT OF HIM, AS LARGE AS HIS OWN HEAD, AND THEN 3 BOWLS IN FRONT OF HIM.

THEN WE SEE AN IMAGE OF A QUEEN/KING IN FINERY, EATING THREE BIG BOWLS OF PINK PUDDING.

MEANWHILE A GENTLE MOTHER-SON CONVERSATION IS GOING ON:

JONATHAN

Why can't I have more pudding Mummy?

MUM

We can't afford more than one packet for pudding.

JONATHAN

Can the Queen afford three packets, mummy?

MUM

I expect she can but it would make her fat to eat all that.

JONATHAN

Does she go to buy Instant Whip for a special treat like we do?

MUM

I expect she's got special ways to buy them and a special place to store them

JONATHAN

I bet she's got a room full of Instant Whip packets at her palace!

WE SEE JONATHAN'S SPOON SLIDING INTO THE WHIPPED PUDDING AND SUCKING UP A BIG DOLLOP, THEN JONATHAN'S HAND TURNS AND LETS IT DROP BACK INTO THE BOWL.

EXTERIOR

JONATHAN'S FACE, STILL RUNNING, HE LICKS HIS LIPS AS IF HIS MOUTH IS WATERING AT THE THOUGHTS.

INTERIOR

WE SEE HIM AT THE BOWL AGAIN, SLIDING HIS SPOON OVER THE TOP OF THE CREAM AND PUTTING IT TO HIS MOUTH. THEN HE IS SCRAPING THE BOWL AROUND AND PICKING IT UP TO LICK IT. MEANWHILE THE SOUNDS HAVE HASTENED ..

EXTERIOR

WE SEE JONATHAN COLLIDE WITH A MAN ON A BIKE, UNSEEN PREVIOUSLY, HEADING FROM THE

OTHER HILL BESIDE THE CROSSROADS. BOTH LAND IN A HEAP SO YOU CAN'T TELL WHO IS WHERE AND THE BICYCLE WHEEL SPINS FAST AS THE CLATTERING DIES AWAY TO SILENCE.

JONATHAN

Ouch. . . . . . Mum . . . Mummy!

THE MAN ON THE BIKE IS JUST A HUMP RISING FROM THE MUDDLE OF SPINNING WHEELS AND LOOSE PEDAL. THE BOY IS RUBBING HIS KNEE.

MAN

Oh. Drat it! Steady on boy. What you . . .

WE SEE HIS ELDERLY FACE AND THEN HIS WRINKLED DITHERY HAND REACHES OUT TO THE BIKE HANDLE.

JONATHAN (DEFENSIVE)

Oooh. My knee . . . Oh Oh Sorry

WE SEE JONATHAN BEND TO TOUCH HIS SANDAL, BUT LEAVE IT. IT IS HANGING FROM THE STRAP ON HIS ANKLE. HE IS BREATHLESS AND FRIGHTENED. WITHIN A MOMENT THE MAN AND THE BIKE ARE DISENTANGLED, AND THE MAN LETS OUT A HEAVY SIGH

MAN

You all right lad?

JONATHAN

Yeh. I . . . . I'm . . .

MAN

Nothin' that won't heal. You need brakes on them legs of yours.

JONATHAN

I got brakes.

MAN

Lucky I wasn't a car. You'd have been dead.

JONATHAN

(MAKING TO CONTINUE RUNNING IN URGENCY.) Going shopping, see.

HE REMEMBERS THE MONEY IN HIS POCKET AND SLAPS IT, URGENTLY.

INTERIOR

WE SEE A FLASH OF THE IMAGE OF HIS PUDDING.

MAN

Go along then.

Do as y'mum says and don't run down the hill.

JONATHAN RUNS AWAY. IN HIS HEAD WE HEAR HIM WONDERING:

JONATHAN

How does he know what Mummy says?

NOW WE SEE AND HEAR JONATHAN WALKING TOWARD A SHOP SIGN, HIS SANDAL STILL FLOPPING ABOUT ON HIS FOOT. HIS KNEES ARE GRAZED.

HE LOOKS CLOSELY AT THE PALMS OF HIS HANDS, THEY ARE GRAZED AND PITTED WITH GRIT.

WE SEE HIS FACE IN ANGUISH AND CLOSE TO TEARS.

THE MAN CYCLES PAST, WAVING IN REASSURANCE.

JONATHAN

Instant whip. Instant. Carrots . . . Um . .

HE STOPS AND THINKS AND TURNS, AND RUNS BACK TOWARD THE HILL AND HIS HOUSE. THE MONEY STILL JANGLES IN HIS POCKET.

WE SEE THE TOP OF THE HILL AND THE HOUSES AND MUM STANDING, ARMS FOLDED AND ANXIOUS. MUM IS WEARING A LONG, GATHERED SKIRT WHICH IS BILLOWING IN THE WIND. HER

BARE ARMS REACH OUT AS JONATHAN APPROACHES. WE HEAR HIS BEATING HEART AND SOBBING. MUM LOOKS DISTRAUGHT AND CATCHES THE BOY AS HE RUSHES AT HER, CRYING LOUDLY AND SHAKING.

JONATHAN

I forgot . . . I forgot . . . . What you wanted and . . . . and . . . . and there was a Man . . .

THE BIRD'S EYE VIEW GETS FURTHER AND FURTHER AWAY AS THE CREDITS RISE.

ENDS

© Bernie Ross, 2000

Now - if you haven't already - read the simple vignettes to see how the pictures have been added to make it a film script.

Read Vivid Prose

Always try to read books and stories that paint mental pictures, and avoid the literature of comment, opinion and 'telling', such as is found in many newspapers. If you want to improve the visual effects in your output, then you must be conscious of imbibing good quality literature too.

You will learn to create images by writing what you see, observing things closely, thinking about how you might put the picture into words. Make these thoughts a habit and a way of life.

Like everything in writing, you just keep trying, and practice will make it nearly perfect.

Plots and Predicaments

'Plot' used to frighten me. Plot was beyond me.

I wanted to write stories so I set about learning what I needed to know. As a new writer, many years ago, I felt a little disappointed and insulted to realise that all I'd gained through reading stories was planned! It was plotted!

Where was the artistic expression? Where the catharsis? It was as if the magical potion in the books I'd lived with, turned out to be a conventional drug that had been prescribed, when I could've bought it over the counter.

I hated - and still hate - the idea of planning a story before I write it. However, now that I know what it is, I no longer feel afraid of it, and I can put 'plot' aside and start writing what I want.

Write What You Want to Say

Plot revolves around character. Without character, there is no plot. A character wants something and his efforts to get it are thwarted by one, two, or several hurdles.

More characters have their own agendas. What they want intrudes upon the main character's goal. Conflicts are many and the plot is formed by the closure of the loop: in a simple story the end ties up nicely with the main character getting what he wanted.

James Bond achieves his mission through winning successive physical and mental battles with his enemies; and because we've all grown to like him he gets to sleep with the beautiful girl. This latter point is very important because it respects the emotional attachment the audience has with the main character. Without acknowledging the reader's feelings, a story is little more than a news report.

When you understand plot, you can write without plotting. Even the best-laid plans go wrong sometimes, so remember and embrace the idea that stories often change in the telling. That's okay, swim with it.

In the beginning

The reader wants to know straight away:- who is my friend in this story? Good characterisation is at the heart of any plot. That means you must create someone whose dialogue (Talk & Tell) is believable. You want the reader to visualise (Visualisation) the character, and you want the reader to care (Get a Life! Emotions and Arguments) enough to read on.

So how do you start? The easiest way is to pretend the concept is already in existence. The concept is the character and his goal, or the event that you envisage. Well it probably is in existence in your mind. Simply start writing the bit that most interests you.

This will mean your story begins in the thick of the first conflict. You might even find yourself describing the absolute climax of the drama. That's okay. Whatever excites you will come over as exciting to the reader.

Now examine what you've written. Answer the questions; not by explaining, but by showing this important information. Expand on the detail, where the pace can take it. Pace would become non-existent with explaining something like this:

> 'John was still in his underpants when he chased and attacked the thief. The robber fought and bit and scratched John. This was because Janet had been repairing his track suit where it was split when climbing a tree two days ago.'

For goodness sake find a way of illustrating it in another way. Perhaps

> John's underpants snagged on the window as he leapt out. The robber was making for the gate, clutching an armload of booty; the hi-fi leads trailing behind. John clambered off the balcony and down

the tree. He looked for his tracksuit hanging near the kitchen window, lest Janet had finished repairing it, but no - too late. Now the robber was trapped at the gate so John grabbed the linen pole . . .

There are ways of showing vital snippets of information and that's what makes story writing such fun. Actually Janet had burned John's tracksuit because he insisted on wearing it to work when all the other Members of Parliament looked so smart.

Writing the middle

It's awfully tempting to start filling in the histories and the flashbacks, but then the middle of your story will sag. Every hurdle needs to build on the character and make him all the more believable, increasing the reader's empathy. That means the story must move. Matters get better or matters get worse. The goal is as important as life or death.

Here is where additional emotions are considered. Somewhere you have to establish what would be the norm. The plot is a digression from status quo but if the readers can't gather what would have been usual (status quo), the emotional impact won't take effect.

If a woman cries every day at the sound of a cabbage being cut, then it's nothing unusual if she cries at the sight of a severed cauliflower head.

However, if she has spent ten years trying to grow the perfect cauliflower and this one looked as if it would grow to competition quality, then we understand and empathise with her crying at the sight of it being cut.

Will she retaliate? Will she go on to grow another? Will she stop crying at the sound of cutting cabbages because nothing will ever be as upsetting as the sight of her severed cauliflower? Will a handsome prince bring her a magic cauliflower to take to the competition? The plot thickens, because another character, with another goal, is getting involved.

Plots thicken even further when goals turn out to need a different or unexpected method of pursuit. A plot will be thicker and more interesting if certain characters are not what they appear to be (remember the blind spots we talked about in Get a Life!), or if they have an ulterior motive. Some of the most satisfying stories to read, and yet the most challenging to write, are those where the 'unreliable narrator' shows the way. The unreliable narrator says one thing but means something else. It's a very clever, experienced writer who can make it work.

Writing the end

Beginner's stories often fall down at the end. You don't want it to be predictable so you invent a twist, or the conclusion fails to tie up with the main character's goal. Then the structure is askew.

As a story reader you want to be satisfied, feel pleased with yourself or pleased for the character's achievement. A pleasing ending for the new writer might resemble a fairytale where the frog turns into a prince or vice versa. Trick endings, twist endings, magic or suicide - write it if you must; but then think again. There's a good ending waiting to be written. All you must do is find it.

A Tidy and Logical Tale

A good ending will see to it that the protagonist, your main character, gets what he wanted. If he doesn't, he needs to find an acceptable or better outcome. If the end of your story doesn't involve the same protagonist that was seeking a goal at the beginning, then your story has no structure. The loop isn't closed, the goal isn't met, the problem isn't solved. Here's an example:

1) I want a car for my birthday so that I can visit

my sisters.
2) I try saving the money, but that has to be spent on a new central heating system instead.
3) I send a brilliant entry to a competition, but someone else wins the money.
4) I meet a rich person who wants to buy me a car.
5) They don't like me going out so they buy me a summerhouse instead of a car.
6) The rich person - with whom I am now in love - condemns all cars and I agree they are pollutants. We condemn all car owners, and ban cars from our home.
7) I'm so appalled at car owners' polluting ways that I refuse to even have a lift in a car to see my sisters.

This wouldn't be a sound plot because there's no satisfaction in the end. However, if -

8a) My sisters turned up in a car at the end and I turned them away because of my beliefs -

Then the story would work, but with adjustment. I'd have to amend the emphasis at the beginning to say: I want to go visit my sisters and the only way I can think of doing so is to have my own car. This implies the only reason I want to visit them is that I'm lonely and haven't got a special friend.

The endings (7 or 8a) would then work because I've got the friendship I need and no longer want to visit my sisters even if I could drive myself to see them. The emphasis moved to loneliness in the beginning and to its relief at the end.

An alternative, preferable end might be -

8b) I visit my sisters on the train.

This would work without an adjustment because my goal;

to visit my sisters, is met. The arrival on the scene of the rich person with strong views is instrumental in giving me the money, confidence, or encouragement I needed to go visit them via train. The ending ties up with the goal made known in the beginning.

If the above example has confused you, take it as warning. You can play forever with combinations of emotions and events to make stories. Many hours have been spent doing so, and many stories have been rejected for not tying up neatly.

It is best to aim for an uplifting end to your story, especially if it's a short-story, and particularly if you want to aim it at the women's magazine market.

Sad endings do work if they are satisfying for the reader and if they bring a wrongful character to a rightful justice. In this instance 'wrongful' means disliked by the readers, so you see how important it is to gauge the reader's emotional responses to every character in your story.

Predicaments

The great thing about writing is that it helps you explore certain situations in order to understand them better. When I first read Georges Polti's 36 Dramatic Situations for stories I felt completely stupid.

"What is this bloke on about?" I said. Here, I hope to give you the benefit of my hard-earned insight.

First you must interpret the archaic language to something meaningful to you. Then - to help it grow into a story plot - you must give the situation to a character with whom you and the readers feel strong empathy.

> 1. Supplication. A humble request. My son-in-law took my daughter into the woods and humbly requested her hand in marriage. What if - she'd said "No"?

2. Deliverance. Rescued from death or danger. Superhero tried to save the maiden but she resisted. If she returned to the sea from which the helicopter plucked her, she'd become a mermaid once more.
3. Crime pursued by vengeance. Committing a crime through taking revenge. "When you hate someone it doesn't mean you can break their toys," said Tommy's mother. "No, and you can't go shoplifting just because the proprietor's a millionaire," said Dad to Tommy's sister.   Later, Tommy and his sister planned a murder campaign on their parents, but the shopkeeper found them out.
4. Vengeance taken for kindred upon kindred. Revenge shown for one friend, against another. I set out to reprimand Julia's husband for his misdemeanours, and yet Julia stopped me in my tracks. "If he's cited with the other woman then I have good grounds for divorce!" she said, and I decided to go along with her plan. It would set her free to marry me, after all.
5. Pursuit. The chase or hunt. Peter followed the woman wherever she went, offering chocolates, opening doors. Ultimately it was his smile that won her over, and they married with an old fashioned church service with finery: for which Peter had always prayed.
6. Disaster. An accident or act of God.
7. Falling prey to cruelty or misfortune. Victim of cruelty or bad luck
8. Revolt. Rebellion.
9. Daring enterprise. Courageous adventure.
10. Abduction. Kidnap or run away with.
11. The enigma. A mysterious happening.
12. Obtaining. Gaining possession or achieving.
13. Enmity of kinsmen. Hostility toward relation by blood or marriage.
14. Rivalry of kinsmen. Competition with a

relative.
15. Murderous adultery. Premeditated killing of spouse for sex.
16. Madness. Insanity and its affect on others.
17. Fatal imprudence. Death through carelessness.
18. Involuntary crimes of love. Instinctive law-breaking for love.
19. Slaying of a kinsman unrecognised. Killing a relative without knowing.
20. Self-sacrifice for an ideal. Perfection upheld above personal safety.
21. Self-sacrifice for kindred. Relative or friend before personal safety.
22. All sacrificed for passion. Emotional rapture takes first place above all.
23. Necessity of sacrificing loved ones. Forfeiting loved ones for an even greater need.
24. Rivalry of superior and inferior. Conflict or competition with a better or worse person.
25. Adultery. Voluntary sex with another's spouse.
26. Crimes of love. Premeditated law-breaking for love.
27. Discovery of the dishonour of a loved one. Victim of adultery.
28. Obstacles to love. People, places, circumstances hindering family or romantic love.
29. An enemy loved. Define your enemy, then seek the nice bits.
30. Ambition. A strong desire to succeed.
31. Conflict with a god. Mental or physical battle against a supreme image or being.
32. Mistaken jealousy. Wrongly fearing a rival winning the object of your desire.
33. Erroneous judgement. Making a mistake.
34. Remorse. A guilty conscience, with shame.
35. Recovery of a lost one. Finding someone

you thought was lost.
36. Loss of loved ones. Deprived by accident or forfeit, of a loved one.

Use a great deal of lateral thinking on the above 'situations'. They will come into their own when given to sound, strong characters; and will be especially intriguing when the situations cross one over another.

With each idea you pursue, consider the degree of drama necessary because a situation is only as important and relevant as it is to the character.

Look at other Ways

Another way of building an idea into a plot is by using your imagination with everyday proverbs.

Here are a few to get you thinking : -

> Only dead fish swim with the tide
> A good name is sooner lost than won
> Great oaks from little acorns grow
> Discontent is the first step in progress.
> A burnt child dreads the fire
> Only the wearer knows where the shoe pinches

The Structures of Novels

Most novels have a shape, and if you think 'visually' you will probably be able to draw a shape that illustrates the structure, as you see it. The shape of a novel will be different for every individual, but most people will agree that there needs to be a high point in the story. It doesn't necessarily follow that there should be a low point, but the story is sure to be better if it plunges the reader into a despair before raising the spirits, excitement, expectation, or emotional intensity.

In a mystery, the high point is in discovering the answer. In a romance, the high point is the eventual union. In a horror story, the high point is probably the ghastly climax. In a joke, the high point is the punch line.

Without a struggle, the challenge seems insignificant :- no story develops.

There are anecdotes, there are jokes, there is storytelling, there is factual history and there is fiction. If you want to write stories you must concentrate on the latter definition, because fiction gives a reader a mental movie, without the tedious explanation.

You can explain a story to someone as a synopsis. Try this: Girl meets boy, girl falls in love with him, boy goes away to work, girl writes endless unanswered letters, and after her extra efforts he finds out she has the wrong address, responds after all, and happiness results from their re-union.

This is a story but it isn't fiction. It is an outline - and not a very good one - of a screenplay, or book or stage play or whatever. You would soon be falling asleep if a whole book were written in telling language like that.

A good short story creeps over you like a warm, silent tide. It engages your emotions to such an extent that you forget who you are, momentarily, and you forget that it isn't true. The way to engage readers so completely that they forget themselves, lies in your ability to create a believable image and emotion. Whether you ultimately hope to write fiction or non-fiction, then understanding how a good story works enables you to invent a compelling piece of literature.

Think of the following as a stairway;

> Start
> Girl meets boy
> Girl falls in love
> Boy goes away
> Girl writes once - no answer
>   Girl writes again - no answer
>   Girl writes again - no answer
> Girl phones
> Boy answers phone
> United in romance, they live happily ever after.

It's a simple story but it only requires a reader to keep reading if we care about the girl in the first place. (Reading the outline, we don't care.)

This is a terribly simple construction: weave together several sequences of basic elements like these to create something more complex and demanding, and remember - character is all important - the reader has to care.

Look to Your Experience

You've probably experienced enough problems in your life to be able to disguise any of them as fiction. However, you don't remember them (and - yes - you should've kept a diary), and those you do recall are simply too close and too difficult or embarrassing to write.

This is where problem pages are really useful. They are distant enough; they involve a 'really worried' character with whom you can probably empathise; and the situation is ideal for constructing into a plausible story.

Vignettes often develop into a story. See how 'First Errand' (in Vignettes) became a short screenplay, in the chapter called Visualise.

A simple hunger pang in Brian Baker brought forth a well-structured story about Bananas during the post-war ration period. In 'The First' Brian has created a frame for numerous stories. The goal for each is clear - I think it works well.

The First - by Brian Baker

It happened again last night.

Comfort feeding they call it. Not hungry, just something to fill the commercial break.I selected a banana from the bowl of fruit, peeled away the skin ... and tasted my childhood.

I recalled the spread of rumour, "Some shops have them"; the frustration of delay, "Martin Young's had one already"; and the thrill as Mother handed me one of my own: my very first banana.

We youngsters had grown up with the war, so knew no other life, but even we could hardly fail to notice how things were changing, now that it was over. We no longer had to carry gas masks wherever we ventured, air raid shelters became places to explore and play in, sea defences were being removed, mines lifted and the beaches opened for our adventures.

The cessation of the war also heralded an increase in world trade, now that ships could again sail the oceans, safe from bombs, mines and submarines. We showed little interest when this was translated into extra rations of meat, butter, cheese and sugar, but whooped with joy when our sweet coupons were suddenly worth four ounces, instead of the customary two ... Yes, life was changing, but slowly.

Then that rumour swept through the school, "Some shops have bananas!" We waited with baited breath to see if it were true. Yes, it was, and Mother proved it by handing me one for my breakfast. I touched it, smelt it, and asked how to eat it. Mother showed me how to unzip it, gave me a couple of slices of bread to eat with it and stood back . . grown-ups didn't get them you see: there were not enough to go round.

What a meal that was. I nibbled and licked, smelt and savoured, consuming barely an inch for my breakfast; then re-sealed it for dinner time. Another inch vanished at dinner; sliced thinly and smothered in custard: delicious. Dashing home from school that afternoon I found my treasure was brown and wilted, but ideal to crush and spread upon yet more bread and butter. Then I scraped the pith from inside the skin, added a sprinkle of sugar, and prolonged that exotic taste on yet another slice of bread. Wow, three meals from a single banana; and each a feast, worthy of a war hero.

Banana stories proliferated at that time, some children were said to have been sick from eating them, others were frightened by them, a few traded them for equally scarce chewing gum or chocolate ... you would be amazed at the purchasing power of a nicely curved banana!

My favourite story concerned a young boy: the first at his school to receive one. He displayed his curved golden beauty in front of his classmates, reveling in his moment of fame. He allowed his admirers to touch it, but drew the line when they asked for a share. As pressure mounted he could see that interest was turning to envy. In the nick of time he dashed to the Boys Toilet and locked himself in. Within minutes he returned, licking his fingers and extolling the flavour.

"Can I have the skin?" asked an envious little girl.

"Skin," repeated our banana connoisseur. "What skin....?" ©Brian Baker 2001

[Brian Baker is a Writing Life® student of long standing. He lives in Colchester, England and his writing is directed towards a six-volume journey through a year of his life. This includes 365 stories recounting gems like his first parachute jump; the death of two German airmen in WW2; the birth of his two children; the loss of friends; the first snowflake to settle; his favourite pub; and sharing every kiss he has enjoyed.]

When I spoke to Brian about his story and the way it is sculpted into a shape where no shape existed, he seemed nonplussed. "I just wrote it," he said.

That says it all - don't get hung-up on plotting.

There are numerous ways to write a story with a plot and without further ado you should simply try it.

For simplicity and in summary:-

> 1) Take us to the location. Give us a friend, and give us a reason to stay with him or her.
> 2) Describe physical attributes, and visual images involved in the story. Show things going on, show things going wrong, and ideals that are out of reach. Don't be afraid of being melodramatic because you can tone it down after.
> 3) Go with the flow. Let it write itself. The characters will take control but do keep the main character's goal in mind. Focus on one viewpoint or you could get in a tangle. Too many focal points means there'll be no focus at all.
> 4) Control the background ideas, history, and essential development. Know these things yourself (and if not, write about them to explore them) but keep the description out of your story. Show it through dialogue or evidence, but don't tell it because this kills the drama. Pinpoint the essential element from the background to give it to some characters as a shared experience.

For example: Someone saying, "Oh, heavens! You're wearing that dress!" could open up a whole can of worms to be talked about. (The story of the dress being the background 'can of worms'.) Similarly a birthday card or losing a piece of sentimental value jewellery can be enough to introduce the relevant past. Keep the author's voice out of it!

An introduction to a past element of the story enriches the character, making it all the more believable. This is especially so if it shows the other side of the character - one which might be instrumental in the story's ending.

> 5) Tie up the loose end and stop. Rewrite and edit many, many times; leaving it a few days between each revisit. (With a small story that I wrote quite 'easily', I actually edited it 20 times or more.) For a short story ensure that every word counts toward showing the single incident, or moving it toward its natural end.

Don't try to run before you can walk. Writing a successful story takes practice, so even if your notes and observations don't immediately strike a story plot, everything you write, anytime, will be valuable in the long run.

The Creative Process

"Every child is an artist, the problem is how to remain an artist as a grown up" Pablo Picasso

Painfully addictive and yet beautiful, the creative process is different for everybody.

As Picasso says, we are all artists. I know I was born to write but those who come to it late in life soon become drawn into its powerful 'otherness'.

"The true artist will let his wife starve, his children go barefoot, his mother drudge for his living at seventy, sooner than work at anything but his art."*G.B. Shaw*

Writing adds a dimension to your life that you cannot always see until you do it. Brain to pen, thoughts in your hand, concepts on paper or screen and translated back to become real. It's magic. Some people say it's miraculous, that it is God at work, that writing or painting or creating is a spiritual experience.

A Big Responsibility

The thought is frightening. It's frightening enough to make you stop short of ever making a start. But make a start you must, you know it. There will be no peace in your mind until you've attempted to express something, even if you don't know what to say, or whether to write it, paint it, sing it or play it to an audience.

"How can I know what I think until I see what I say?" *E.M. Forster*

It doesn't help to hear so-called experts talking highly of painters and writers and playwrights who've "got something to say" and you look at their masterpiece and wonder quite what. You see the artwork of great painters like Jackson Pollock or Piet Mondrian, installations by Tracy Emin or

Damien Hirst - only to look upon them and say "What?"

Believe me - you've got things to say and by getting that pen moving you'll start to find out what they are. You have to find your way of working, whether it's with a pen, a typewriter, pencil, computer; the side of the phone book, the back of a shopping list, a pristine new notepad or a perfect white screen with a spell-check and thesaurus at the click of a mouse. It won't be easy, but you can make it easier for yourself - if you'll accept that pampering your creativity is a worthy cause.

Brought Home and Privately Yours

You can write in weird and wonderful ways, observe the world and quietly write what you see. It might be fictionalised reality, but seen from your standpoint, with your unique eye and in your own words, it will say something to your readers that'll give them one more viewpoint from which to understand.

> "I wish I were more at home with writing. I can go a year or two or three without picking up my pen and I'm perfectly content. The minute I have to write I become neurotic and grouchy and ill; I become like a little wet, drenched bird, and I put a blanket over my shoulders and I try to write and I hate myself and I hate what I'm writing." said Edmund White, American novelist and author of the acclaimed 'A Boy's Own Story' (1982).

I was lucky enough to be brought up by an artist and learned to understand the necessity to accommodate the neurotic, grouchy and ill side of the temperament. The only time it would surface was when life and circumstances stood in the way of my father's Creative Process. Unfortunately for me and for the rest of the family, that was quite often.

Accommodate Your Destiny

You either grow up to do as your parents did, or you do the opposite. I hope I do the opposite - I recognise my need to create and try to engineer everything to ensure my Creative Process takes precedence. Lack of confidence and lack of being accepted by the art establishment curtailed my father's artistic focus, but having four children didn't help. However, my feet developed well in hand-me-down shoes, and my needs are modest, thanks to my father's teachings. It is just as well, because creating my art, writing, doesn't pay well, and I've learned not to waste my time on doing anything else.

"I don't believe for a moment that creativity is a neurotic symptom. On the contrary, the neurotic who succeeds as an artist has had to overcome a tremendous handicap. He creates in spite of his neurosis, not because of it," said Aldous Huxley.

This man may well be famous for his experiments with drugs but he created numerous stories, poems, novels, plays, travel works, historical studies and academic essays.

"I loathe writing," says Muriel Gray. "It's hard, hard work, like digging the roads… " she says in her interview with David Mathew in The Third Alternative, no. 27. (www.TTAPress.com)

You'll probably know her as a TV and BBC Radio presenter but of writing she says, "There's no comparison to broadcasting work which is basically money for old rope." Writing is her passion and, it seems, her reason for living. Her latest book is The Ancient (pub. Harper Collins, £9.99)

Pain is no barrier

"A writer is somebody for whom writing is more difficult than it is for other people," said Thomas Mann.

James Baldwin does a lot of rewriting. "It's very painful."

All writers and artists talk of the pain but if you're wise you'll accept that it's going to be painful. It has so often been compared to giving birth that it's hardly worth mentioning - but when you're pregnant, you know, it's a hell of a relief to experience that pain; and look at the beautiful reward!

It isn't funny to have to put up with any pain at all, and to have writers' block when you know you want to do it; but there are so many jokes about it.

This one sums it up for me:

> 1ST WRITER (at a cocktail party): I'm working on my new novel.
>
> 2ND WRITER: Neither am I.

Quoted from Private Eye in The Writer's Chapbook, ed. George Plimpton.

Find a Way

How do you accommodate your need to create? How do you make it least painful? If it's ideas or a starting point you need then go to the Triggers chapter, or Therapy, or find your voice in Write with Style, or even in the zany Experimental ideas.

Perhaps it's the place and the company you keep that curtails your outflow? Teachers of old who stood behind you to pounce on your mistakes have a lot to answer for. But you're free of that now and only have to be wary of imposing your own inhibitions.

> J.K. Rowling sat in a café to write the Harry Potter books. Maybe it was to keep warm and topped up with coffee but your reason might be different: if it works for you, do it.

> Brenda Crowe wrote 'Play is a Feeling' and 'Living with a Toddler' sitting up in bed: not because she was ill or working at night, but

because it was the best way to keep her feet warm.

Julian Stockwin writes the Kydd series at his desk accompanied by an ancient piece of mariner's rope, which wafts the subtle fragrance of the deep sea.

Jack Kerouac would kneel to pray before starting to write his novels ('On the Road', 1957; 'The Subterraneans',1958 et al) and in essays he outlined a philosophy of writing that refused all revision and was akin to improvisational jazz.

The poet Philip Larkin would say he never went out, while Nadine Gordimer thinks writers should do plenty of ordinary things to keep in touch with life. She says, "The solitude of writing is also quite frightening. It's quite close sometimes to madness, one just disappears for a day and loses touch. . . ."

When you've 'been there' - felt the solitude of being a writer - you know why emails and web sites like author.co.uk are so essential for helping you stay mentally buoyant.

Love It or Hate It

"I love writing," said P.G. Wodehouse. "I never feel comfortable unless I am either actually writing or have a story going. I could not stop writing."

He was the author of the Jeeves Series and very successful in musical comedy, theatre, and Hollywood.

This quote is encouraging for me personally. At a recent workshop I found myself - in an automatic writing exercise - writing and then reading aloud: "I only feel well when I'm writing." This produced gasps from a quarter of the other students. They were people who were still hoping to find out why or how writing can change their lives for the better.

Now before I make the mistake of offering the creative process as a religion, I think I will assume that my readers know they do want to write, but haven't yet decided on their niche. We look at this with some general ideas in Genres.

Do Your Own Thing

There is nothing unusual in wanting to do your own thing.

> Lawrence Durrell says this: "It doesn't really matter whether you're first rate, second rate, or third rate, but it's of vital importance that the water finds its own level and that you do the very best you can with the powers that are given you."

Lawrence Durrell was a poet, travel writer and prolific novelist; and not to be confused with his brother Gerald who wrote of animal life and owned a zoo at Jersey.

Reading the candid comments of other writers is an eminently useful way of endorsing your urge to write.

> "The most essential gift for a good writer is a built-in, shock-proof shit detector. This is the writer's radar and all great writers have had it." Ernest Hemingway said.

He was one of the greatest short story writers of America and won the Nobel Prize for Literature in 1954. This is bestowed for 'the most outstanding work of an idealistic tendency' and was awarded for The Old Man and the Sea, first published in 1952. "I learn as much from painters about how to write as from writers," he said. Have a go with Creative Frolics and see if you can see what he means. I think I can: you'll see I have a tendency to cross the paths of painters in some suggestions on the Experimental page.

Finding your niche, your style, your way of working, can only be done through time and experience. Writing a diary and writing vignettes gives you a body of work that will be an endless supply of material to adapt or rewrite - along with many embellishments and an ever-strong urge to extend your vocabulary.

What of the Process, once Established?

Ian McEwan, talks about being 'haunted' by ideas that culminated in his latest novel 'Atonement'. "It caused me a lot of anxiety," he says in an interview with Will Cohu (Daily Telegraph 22.9.2001). "I kept worrying I was going to screw it up." His writing process is compared to a kind of landscape gardening, acknowledging 'a passion for the aesthetic as much as the organic'.

I regard myself as an organic writer, perhaps in the same way as McEwan, perhaps not. I encourage my students to write organically - as if the first sentence is a stem, and from that will grow roots and shoots, flowers and seeds. It is sure to grow if you plant it as words on paper or screen.

I write stories and plays (including TV scripts and screenplays), and the odd poem, in between the mainstay of creative non-fiction, which you're reading now. All can be written in an organic way.

For the record: what are my writing habits? I write words and half-sentences in notebooks, between doing other things; I start early, in solitude at the computer or just at a table. I break to make myself tea (eight cups a day). I do housework and cooking between paragraphs, and scribble beginnings, usually, in bed in the dark.

I think the creative process is all about making connections, and building upon them. (See Visualise for more on this.) There's the 'What If - ?' game; but by building simple tentative connections into something bigger, there's a worthy point to be made. I rely on dreams and on the half-sleep images that dwell in my head. They conveniently solve problems for me. Yesterday I was wondering how to explain my difficulties with defining Visualisation for this text. Overnight I dreamt about the picture I tried to paint, long ago, called Rhapsody in Black. Today I used it to illustrate the problem: my memory, my connection, was already there, I just had to find the right place to use it.

If you want to read more about my writing philosophy then Creative Writing the Organic Way will give you greater insight. It is available as the course material for Writing Life®

Try any and all ways, methods, outlets and keep at it. Experimental; Vignettes; Genres. The creative process that suits you will make itself known. This way, your writing will command respect as well.

Experimental Writing

*"You have to play with words and ideas, speak them
and feel them in your mouth, see them on paper
and feel them shimmering in your bones."*

Doing a few experiments with new and old ideas will undoubtedly provide a spot of refreshment. Before a stage play opens to the public, the director will have the actors trying different voices, moods and methods for the piece, to ensure the best performance goes out. As writers, we can play with our material too.

Scrape the Barrel

Funnily enough, it is often when you're delving your pits for ideas that your best writing emerges. If nothing comes of the work, well it was simply good practice. These are not word games: some of the following ideas have proven to produce my favourite or most valued pieces of work, and they've kicked many a creative writer into progress.

Surrealist Picture

Find a surrealist painting such as Salvador Dali's The Persistence of Memory, or Woman with a Head of Roses, and describe it in full and glorious detail. Shelve it separate from the picture and when you read it another time, you'll think "Wow! What's going on?" Some great prose!

Capture a Pose

"Mother and Child" or "Woman kneeling on chair". Outdoors near a park bench, or at home with your loved ones, describe the character(s) and their pose. Be an artist, sketching with words.

Write Graffiti

Use an old phone book or newspaper, and a thick black marker, or paint or crayon that's really bright. Write boldly and madly on consecutive pages. Give yourself a theme: Birthday; Wedding; Shopping; Money; That Swine of a Spouse. Close the book and hide it from yourself. 3 weeks later, type up the contents.

Take Liberties

Apply something totally taboo to a situation you'd normally respect. School ceremony, strict inspection, a stuffed shirt board-meeting:- ripe for imaginative embroidery. Make it work in words.

Write Blind

We've all written in the dark dead of night before, but have you tried it in daylight at the computer? Set up a blank document and simply switch off the monitor. Write straight to keyboard non-stop. When you turn the monitor back on you'll find it eerie to revisit that 'dream state' - especially if you've never been a touch typist.

Turning Ditties

Write a ditty. Write the same again with a changed word or two. Repeat over and over with a small change every time. See where it takes you - a song, a poem, a novel idea? - for example;

>   Brown bird twittering
>   Falling on its beak
>   Crown bird wittering
>   Balling on its beak
>   Drown turd wittering
>   Calling for its week
>   Stupid bird knitting
>   Tall socks made of teak.

Write a Quilt

Like a collection of beautiful scraps of fabric, sewn together with love and precision, quilt-writing takes chosen images to create a fantastic scene. Use the 'quilt' as a backdrop for one of the character studies you've written.

Write an Obscured Cliché

You know the kind of thing - little dog gets lost, search parties sent out, Mrs Gossip causes offence, turns out she'd locked the dog in the shed. All is well. . . . .

Now delete some haphazard statements. Review it. Add a word here and there, especially using words you love - 'quintessential' or 'breathtaking' or 'gorgonzola' and others. Now revise the whole piece to ensure it makes sense.

Explore Negatives

Make a list of objects: Mountain, tree, necklace, television, bunch of flowers, anything. Write a description of the scene that includes all of them, but do not spell out what they are - simply show their presence.

Write a Sandwich

Make it tasty, or hot; colourful, toasted, or fresh as a cut lettuce. Remember the structure - a sandwich has the two outer layers similarly cushion-like, the butter-sides reversed. The structure of your story or vignette must resemble a closed sandwich.

Mad Metaphors

Collect a handful of images:-

>A turbulent sea
>A box of biscuits
>A beautiful landscape
>A hand-knitted sweater

Football match
Sock drawer

and a handful of concepts:-

Childhood
Knowledge
Parenthood
Music
Relatives
Death
History

Take one from each list at random, and then justify the comparison you have made. The sillier the better.

Ragtime

Write your most boring story in the style of a ragtime song. "C'me on an' sing, come on an' dance, Alexander's ragtime ba - a - and . . ."

She had a face, she had a face, like a fat old saucepan base. And on the day . . On the day . . .

Let the tune and the beat lift away the dour boundaries.

Mirror Dialogue

Talk to yourself in the mirror, recording it on audio tape. Transcribe it to paper or keyboard. Which person isn't quite 'you'? Build on the differences. Build into a story or an argument.

Write a Bike

Describe every nut and bolt, the curves, the shine, the handlebar shape, the aerodynamic design. How do the spokes look as the wheel spins around? How do the chain links grip their respective cog wheels? Detail is good. Look for it and write it.

Write in the voice of...

A renowned politician (if one can be found), a distinctive media presenter or a notable stylist like Arthur Conan Doyle. Try emulating contemporary writers: Booker prize or popular commercial. Voices are for playing with, and rediscovering all the time.

Rewrite a Nursery Rhyme

They started life as real people or anecdotes of true events. Turn one into a modern short story or character study. Go to Talk and Tell (Excerpt from Strange Meeting) for a new interpretation of Jack & Jill's accident on the hill.

Write a Maze

Finally, there are numerous structures for stories but have you ever tried a maze? Draw one, or better still, find one in a puzzle book; and write a story 'following your nose' through the maze. When you reach the right end (or the centre) you'll have learned so much about your subject or character that you might not wish to delete the cul de sacs, but weave them all into a greater whole. Go by instincts when inside the maze, and be brave.

> A trolley appeared and was lined up at her side. The porters lifted; the white cover was removed. The sister held Irena's hand as she slowly moved her head to look.
>
> There lay her daughter. White, perfect, pure and silent, beside her - and dead.
>
> Her little hand was battered and bruised. The mortuary gown concealed a multitude of wounds on the child, just as the white cast mountain which pinned Irena to the bed hid the damage to her own bones.
>
> Irena reached out to touch, but the bare hand was

Find Your Rostrum - Genres

It would be pointless and superficial to try to define every literary genre, not least when 'Literary' is regarded as a genre in its own right.

My philosophy is to write what ever you want to write and then decide - or let others decide - what genre (if any) might best describe it. Creative writing comes in many guises. Formula writing is creative but if you write to a formula it's really up to you to study its rules, conventions and boundaries. If you enjoy the discipline, and many do, then you are welcome.

What a writer needs to do is find the platform that's frequented by the audience who will most appreciate the work. As for me, I move around: the versatility of my writing demands a different rostrum each time. I'm happy with that.

If you, too, are the kind of writer who writes like giving birth and then looks down to see whether it's a boy, a girl, or a monster - well, perhaps the following definitions will help you decide where you're at.

If you feel like a change, perhaps you'll be inspired to write for a new market. Whatever, aiming for a specific genre requires knowledge of its particular conventions. You must study the works you would like to have written yourself.

Here are some brief and personal interpretations, pointing to the idiosyncrasies that seem to stand out:

Creative Non-Fiction

Is what's offered to you on these Writing Focus pages. It acknowledges the use of emphasis on a particular attitude, and there are three elements that define the category:

It is truthful

It is created with artistic vigour

It comes from the writer's heart.

One could say it's emotionally cathartic but I wouldn't want any writer to feel tarred with such a brush. Creative non-fiction takes many forms, from the How To .... article, to the spoof documentary, or the magazine feature that shows you the place and the people along with what was done, said and heard.

Comedy

Can be ridiculous or deadly serious with a truth more poignant than any sad tale. The trick is in violating the audience's expectations.

Crime

Where the main strength and attraction is suspense; and we often have most empathy with the criminal. Good characterisation and emotional pull are what give it strength.

Detective

Where the question is Whodunnit? And our empathy lies with the detective whose problem is to solve it. Readers are looking for clues - who will get it first?

Poetry

Concise and to the point, using the fewest and best words in the best order. Poetry doesn't have to rhyme, and there are numerous definitions to match the 'rules' that some poetry adheres to: sonnets; rhyming couplets; the villanelle; blank verse; free verse; haiku; cinquain; tanka - to name only a few. I, personally, combine poetry and prose, as you'll see in the story 'Can you feel . . . ?'

Stage Plays

The stories focus on relationships that have a history and could happen anywhere, so that dialogue and action are specifically the writer's task. The director can choose to use minimal sets without losing the strength of the play. The web site for the British Theatre and a regular newsletter is - http://britishtheatre.about.com. At www.author.co.uk/perform we plan an event for writing for performance.

Television plays - series & sitcoms

Are where faces matter. Physical expressions can be shown in detail, as can locations and specific details. Must be fast and engrossing or the audience will be lost to another channel. You can subscribe to a new magazine dedicated to scriptwriting on www.TheSWS.co.uk

Film

Similar to TV but the audience is relatively committed so the writer is allowed longer to develop audience empathy with the characters and situations. Also, as with TV and graphic novels, there's potential for epic scenery and special visual and audio effects. The British Film Institute has a web site at - www.bfi.org.uk

Comics - graphic novels

Written rather like films and TV with action, dialogue, and visual shots given separately. Every story must have a moral or a message, and be conducive to visual imagery for the artist.

Horror

Visually gruesome or psychologically disturbing, the climax of the story isn't likely to be for the faint-hearted. It may surprise you to know that sex, blood and cruelty are not compulsory in this genre. See Arguments for a think-piece on writing Horror.

Short Stories

The description covers a multitude of fictions, but all are (or should be) self-contained, strong on structure and character, and encapsulate a novel's worth of message within the exposition of a single incident.

Women's magazine fiction

An art form in itself where emotional matters are illustrated in simple day-to-day events, with an ending that's satisfying and usually uplifting. Tears of joy at the end are preferable to unseemly problems left to linger in the reader's mind. There are some great hints and advice about this market on www.midlandexposure.co.uk

Vignettes

Are described on the Vignettes page where you'll also find some examples. They can live in your head and on paper for years before finding their place in a full work of fiction. By this, their very nature, they are well worth writing and keeping.

Flash Fiction

Flash fiction is the term used for short stories that have a twist or shock at the end - a surprises 'in a flash'. The stories are usually well under 1000 words, perhaps because net-surfers are inclined to move on quickly. The genre is enjoying a rediscovery on the World Wide Web. River Power is a story that could come into this genre. Reading from a screen is rather like listening to a radio play: it is different from reading a book, as you tend not to look back. (The scrolling up and down is so irritating and a roller-ball or wheel on the mouse is a good investment) As with a radio play you carry on, hoping to make sense of it, compelled to find out where the story is going. The flash ending ensures you're not disappointed.

Independent Press

A genre in the sense that it is often eclectic and esoteric. Sometimes I think the various small press magazines are the most literary of all media. They are many and varied in subject matter, and equally so regarding the quality. Study those that appeal to you, offer your work for little or no payment, and keep trying. Get a copy of 'The Fix' from www.TTAPress.com and also check through the list of magazines at author.co.uk.

The list is far from exhaustive. Add your own. Send us your suggestions and brief definitions, with links to examples that might help other writers.

The beauty of the novel

Is that it offers space for thorough examination of psychological matters. It has "the capacity to go into other minds," says Ian McEwan.

The novel can - if worked carefully - provide enlightenment on a subject from more than one character's viewpoint. A good novel or piece of fiction can change your life - see Literary Clout - as can creative non-fiction.

Other Genres

With apologies to aficionados as many of these have a large following;

Science Fiction

Fantasy & Magic Realism

Slipstream

Historical - romance - war - social

Romance

Thrillers - spy - adventure

Ghost Stories

Mystery - whodunnit - psychological trickery

And more.

Then we get to the borderline novels, where one genre doesn't quite describe the content.

Among these I'd include Revenge Tragedy, Black Magic, Urban Gothic . . . Erotica

I didn't wish to omit Erotica from the list as it would then be conspicuous for its absence. Nor did I intend to be denied the opportunity to define the emphasis that once prevailed:- erotica is of the mind, whilst pornography is visual. Alas, now I cannot give these definitions as the boundaries are so blurred.

Romantic Erotica

Women's romantic erotica found particular popularity in the early 1990's. It was a branch of liberation, for women, that was more acceptable to them than the image of the bra-burning feminists of the 70s and 80s.

There was one problem with erotica that brought about its downfall: it cancelled itself out. From the classy, respectable, subtly camouflaged exposition of the passions of love, writers of erotica - and presumably their readers - became impatient and bored. The problem is that sex, in itself, is boring.

Erotica should be sensuous, not sexual; but all good prose is sensual. Most sophisticated novels include the sex scenes anyway, so erotica is a redundant category, certainly for the writer seeking serious literary input and outlets. All good poetry and prose is explicit where the detail, pacing and visual images are vital to the overall effect, so explicit sex comes under the same umbrella.

Here's an example of a short erotic story. The intermittent free verse is intentional.

Can you feel . . . ?

Your eyes are staring into the fumes of surgical spirit and high hopes. Your breath is shallow and immobile, and the whiteness of your flesh is the white of woolpack clouds that is no white at all. You have the serene look of death at your side but won't allow it to roll over and engulf you in its sanctuary. I watch your lips move like the wing of a stunned sparrow, twitching in the wind, fooling an observer. Now I see the bird moving, now I don't and did I ever? Speak to me, speak!

The crisp, starched linen on the high bed puts shame to my sloppy clothes. Your night-dress is in my hand. Soft cotton and perfumed, with dainty embroidered feathers. I would slide it onto you in place of the harsh, yellowed utility gown, if only I could dare to disturb the sterile arrangement which is the nurses' lot. I want you dressed in clothes which spell - and smell of - you. I study your skin, paler and more pure than I ever had pleasure to caress. Soft with white down, so cool and calm. But why won't you look? Why won't you see?

The machinery is humming as if it keeps your heart throbbing. No kidding. Black cables, silver boxes with grey knobs, and tiny red lights which indicate your life. The medics have no real control. They are deluding themselves with their gadgets. You will die when you want to die, I know, and not before. Nor will I let them make you live after.

I hold your hand and scrutinise the creases that tell of your nature. Your ideas. Your garden. Your way of cutting bread. Your supple joints which mix the plaster of Paris again and again or scoop a handful of sculpture and place it at an angle just so. And your fingers still have an outline of white powder round the nail-moons, and your fingernails are jagged and unkempt with repeated turning of clay, chemicals, wire, pliers and wood. Your hands were never akin to the freshness of your complexion or to the buoyancy of every new idea inside your head.

The pain was a concrete barrier - a ball and chain anchoring your zany hopes to the reality of life's mundane spheres. The Ball of Pain was subject to suggestion too:

"This person can cure me!" you said.

> So excited
> to try the magic.
> Spiritual healer. Ethereal assuager.
> With letters after her name.
> A big house. Big gardens.
> Good note paper. Love birds
> in a cage by the front door.

Still here beside you I move your hand, cringing as I find the back of mine touching the mountain of bedclothes which is your wound. At least they knew what they were doing.

> I stop breathing to think
> of the journey to that 'healer'.
> Two pretty girls
> (I am pretty, I am,
> you told me I am.)
> We hitch-hiked
> two maniac males
> in a car made of scrap.
> You were doubled-up in pain,
> but you pretended it was laughter:
> and the walking made you sick.
> And the jolting made you stifle a cry.
> It was a stolen car,
> and your swollen tongue,

was alarming to me
and to anyone who could see.

The giggles turned to tears as reality pulled our senses to a frigid halt. The speed. The stifling petrol from the jalopy, driven beyond its wildest limits. How we ever got out alive I may always regret. That togetherness was all. And still is.

I watched the shamanist woman undress you. Promising a cure. She told you to relax, close your eyes, think of colourful birds in the wild - free and singing in the trees. Across your tummy went her hands, gently at first, stroking and pushing, pummelling the flesh like bread dough. I watched, brimming with hope. And her ecstasy was bewildering, as faster she worked on you, delving into flesh that I'd - never known was there.

Folds of it she found. Folds of your body. You cried out and she hushed you with spiritual psalms and a closing of her heavy black eyelids. The gold crucifix on her neck had a spike at the end. I didn't like it. I didn't like the house. There were toads in every corner: china ones, leather ones. Dried ones. Green ones, brown ones and black.

There was a smell of blood as she operated on you. She called it surgery but there was no opiate even in her voice. Painless now, perhaps numb? The pummelling and delving went on and on, dark blood flowing in rivers around your white stomach, until at last she pulled free - a lump. "The culprit!" she declared. The root of all your pain. The poison growth which made you wince in agony, and here, she announced, was the cause. Removed by the powers of possession through her hands.

Anaesthesia by hope and expectation. Surgery by mind control.

I was sceptical even as she cleaned you. I didn't like the smell. The sight of an uncut wound made me point and almost laugh.

Flippantly, she turned.

"Have you any ailments I can help you with, my dear?"

I shook my head, shocked. Disgusted at her hungry eyes.

So she spoke to you as if I were senseless and mouthless. "Your sister. Your friend, does she need a little prayer too?"

> Cosmetic vacuuming.
> Artificial repair.
> Theatrical miracle.
> It was bullshit.

So we made our way home on foot, uncured, but feeling better if only relieved. Thirty miles.

> Then the pain was even worse.

Bruising, with no visible incision. Disillusioned. Those love birds were miniature ravens.

Grateful millionaires pay the bills with donations and then, thankfully for the vile, violating, trickster, they usually die. How the hell we believed in her cures I'll never know. Tunnel-vision for each other. Safety in the firmness of our love-bond. My adoration sanctioned my every move.

You are not dead nor dying. Your face is white, your mind serene, the new wound in your belly is all sealed up and the bruising is back, but this time it's valid, not pummelled for the sake of effect.

I hold your hand and you move it a little, but I wonder if the numbing drug was too strong to let you ever recover.

    To let you feel anything again:
    The touch of my hand on your cheek.
    The blow of my whisper on your face.

The hair from my fringe when I kiss the bony valleys of your temples, in anticipation of whispering and loving you - tentatively - tenderly - on the trembling nerve-ends in a line down your spine. When you're well.

Slowly, hesitantly, a feather-like touch flowing over your fine down, drawing dimples and craters, pot-holes and molehills, gooseflesh and spikes along the contours toward thy pelvic mound. I want to look at your face and see the tension melting, the creases pronounced in their aim to flesh out and disappear. As the corners of your mouth spread into a contented smile, so will your knees fall effortlessly open and a force beyond words, beyond resistance will pull my fingers to your quim where the healing warmth of love begins to stroke away the pain . . and bring life.

Do you hear me now? Can you feel my presence? My breath and my thoughts. See my shadow even though your eyes refuse to move? Can you taste the foul bitter breath of illness and does it ring true with the smell of Dettol and polish, of hospital dinners and stout black shoes on the dirtless tile floor?

Here: lick the water I place on your lips, it's luke warm and clear as if double-distilled.

It is good. Show me
the life inside your body.
The happiness inside your head.

Tell me now, if there's none. I need to know and to share your death, and brace myself to leave you.

Body and soul; substitute mother; lover and sister and minder.

Can you feel anything when I do this?

© Bernie Ross, 1996

Please note the date. In a desperate attempt to find new ways of saying the same old thing, too much so-called erotic writing in the 21st Century has become littered with over-the-top synonyms, resulting in a plethora of ridiculous euphemisms leading to blatant flesh on flesh. The writing is crude. But if it's crude it isn't erotic, so it has removed itself from the respectable position it held.

The character Fry, in the Futurama cartoon, (a Matt Groening brainchild) summed it up recently in words to the effect: "Thanks to the Internet I'm bored with sex. Now where's the violence?"

I've said for a long time that writing horror (Arguments) is something every writer should tackle so that it's under their belt. When you've written the ultimate (wrenched the depths of your psyche on to the page) then you'll be able to handle absolutely anything in your writing. You'll have set yourself free from internal censors and be you'll able to write things you didn't know were in there, including lively, savage, boundary-pushing prose, television, comedy or more. You'll be able to become a criminal, a child, a mad person or a religious guru, if you're not one of these already. Go to Experimental Writing and see what springs from your mind.

The World Wide Web is teeming with sites about writing, and seems to be hottest on the specialists in Science Fiction and Fantasy. It is no small wonder that boundaries blur when everyone has their own definitions. You just have to keep on reading, writing, and trying.

If something doesn't quite work effectively nor have the impact you intended, it might benefit from being turned to suit another medium, or another genre. At the end of the day it will have taught you a lot about your writing, and it might just find the rostrum that suits you.

Literary Clout

Writers and Philosophy

Writers can put down in words what others want or need to say, but who can't or won't. Our greatest writers have been philosophers (or thinkers) too; though few are recognised as such. What are writers if they don't put their words together to make us think? Writers are observers, they stand apart, take an overview, and can show us all what we are doing whether it's good, bad, ugly, or stupid.

Philosophy is the study of fundamental questions regarding reality, language, the mind, identity, logic, perception, freedom, space, time, and morality. All these can be examined within fictional frameworks, making them more accessible than the academic studies of recognised philosophers. If you can illustrate breathtakingly truthful things in a way that encompasses a strong logical viewpoint within a wide overview, then your writing will have literary clout.

Accessible Writing

Sometimes the most effective philosophic revelations are made through comedy, parody, or symbolism. A writer can find the words to describe examples of behaviour that show the issue for what it is, and gets us all thinking in agreement. Laughter itself is acknowledgement.

The famous philosophers became so well-known because they wrote down their thoughts and presented them to the world. Many writers are philosophers without really knowing it. They think about words even when they're not writing, so it comes more easily to them to present a sound argument in words on a page.

If all that sounds a bit out of your league, read on, because by the end of this article I hope you'll see that you can make good use of your ability with words, even without international acclaim. You, too, can contribute to philosophy.

Be a Grand Inquisitor

The fascinating thing about philosophy is that every subject normally placed under its umbrella tends not to have an answer!

> What is the meaning of life?
> Who is God?
> What is art?
> Is there life after death?
> How did the world begin?

You will have your personal answers to these, and as a writer you'll undoubtedly be able to write statements answering these questions and many more. This is fine - for you. Writing is a tool of thought and it's great for sorting out your own stance on a subject. (See Writing for Therapy.) Yet there is more to it than that.

You can use your gift with words to persuade the population and the powers-that-be to follow an idea that might improve life for many people. You can have clout.

Look at Achievements in the Past

The 'Grapes of Wrath' by John Steinbeck, was written in 1939, when World War II was only beginning. It was a powerful study of the Californian labouring class, and it had a huge affect on the way society thought about slavery.

Within a year he was looking at ways to write some effective propaganda. The result, The Moon is Down, was banned by the Nazis but it so captured the national mood in Norway and other occupied countries, that it sold in tens of thousands. It was made into a play for Broadway and Steinbeck himself, by now also a filmmaker wrote the screenplay.

When asked how he knew so well what the resistance in Norway was doing he said, "I put myself in your place and thought what I would do." Steinbeck was renowned for his sure sense of audience and his empathy with the oppressed.

Simply Empathising

These are skills you can learn. There are some suggestions to play with in the Style chapter as well as in Experimental. Observe, consider, experiment. You, too, can learn to empathise with predicaments (Plots) and pinpoint the sentiments that readers look for in believable fiction.

> Bertrand Russell said: "Three passions, simple but overwhelmingly strong, have governed my life: the longing for love, the search for knowledge, and unbearable pity for the suffering of mankind," in *Autobiography.*

Bertrand Russell and Canon John Collins were instrumental in the launch of CND (Campaign for Nuclear Disarmament) in 1958. Though also a mathematician, Russell was a life long pacifist and spent 6 months in prison for an article he published objecting to the First World War.

Question: What binds each of the following?

> Victor Hugo - French novelist
> Henry George - author of Progress and Poverty
> H.G. Wells - author of The Time Machine, 1895
> Gore Vidal
> William F. Buckley
> Norman Mailer
> Jeffrey Archer

Answer: They have all stood for public office, with varying degrees of success. The list of writers who have dabbled in politics is endless.

Children are free to write and publish what they think because they won't be taken seriously. If they express something that's uncomfortable for those in power then it's generally regarded that "they'll grow out of it". They are easily dismissed. As an adult and experienced writer you can make sure you're not ignored!

We are all free (or like to think we are) to write and publish what we want to say, but there is usually too much at stake for us to take a shocking risk. To lose material wealth or even our lives may be worth it, but on second thoughts, the potential suffering of our loved ones is not.

Your Voice among Thousands

In the week that I'm working on this, the World Trade Centre in New York, along with many thousands of people, was destroyed by terrorists. The shock and knowledge of it is too much for most us to comprehend, and only time can help us. Writers will be the first to get a distance on events and the way the world changes.

Bill Thompson writes in the regular Dispatched Arts Newsletter:

"In the months and years to come it will be through our art that we begin to understand what this all means. As the political and - no doubt - military consequences work themselves out and boundaries are redrawn, battles fought and barriers erected between the west and Islam fundamentalists, the way we think and feel about these changes will be shaped by the responses of our writers and playwrights and painters and sculptors and filmmakers. It will not only come in high-action movies about hijacks and US military might (although we can expect a new Rambo-like figure to emerge in the multiplexes by year's end) but in the way that new paintings quote the tangled metal of the south tower, in the way that New York is written in next year's novels."

Quality of Child Mind

The innocence of childhood is an example to us all, and it's something we could all aspire to. (Go to Liberation and Creative Frolics for a breath of fresh air.) Could you write a novel making the following children's ideals come to life?

In one of Richard & Helen Exley's compilations of children's thoughts, Dear World . .

> An Indian child says, "It should be a compulsory task to produce food. Every man must care for plants."

> "Anyone who goes on strike should be replaced by someone on the dole," says a boy in the UK.

> "Respect women - they are the builders of society," says a boy in Trinidad.

> "If everybody appreciated great people's ideas the world would be better," says Didem Uzumcu, a 15 year old in Turkey.

> "My first rule would be that all sweet firms should be closed down to save money on dental surgery," says an 11 year old in the UK.

The simplicity of children's thoughts is enviable, and as writers we strive to recapture it. We have the advantage (or disadvantage) of wider vision, however. Children's comments reflect their parents' attitudes, or whatever the latest project at school has been covering. This doesn't make their opinion any less valid, but in the balance of things, priority has to go elsewhere. So the sweet companies go on digging gold out of the mouths of babes.

Say What you Think

On a more adult note, Clare Short MP and UK government Minister received more than 5,000 letters of support in her anti-pornography campaigns. Every one of those writers had a personal reason for wanting a ban on the Page 3 Pin-Ups. This one is simple but effective:-

> " I feel there is surely something sick in a society that glorifies (and pays extraordinary amounts for) exposed breasts and yet provides me with a cubicle in a toilet to feed my baby in." Anonymous writer from Sussex

As a writer, will you change the world through a simple definition or letter? It is hard to say what kind of knock-on effect your words might produce, but fear of the unknown shouldn't stop you writing them.

In 1961 Belle Tutaev wrote to the (then) Manchester Guardian suggesting that mothers get together to form small nursery groups: to enhance the children's learning, and to improve the lives of lonely parents. Thus was born the Pre-school Playgroups Association, now known as the PLA (sounds like 'play') - Pre-school Learning Alliance. Forty years on it is an extremely large charity, having shaped many people's lives; now with a powerful influence on Government decisions regarding education and children's welfare, and has a multi-million pound turnover.

Was Belle Tutaev a writer? No, she was a mum, with an urgent need to give mental stimulation to her child and herself.

Be What you Are

What comes first, the study of philosophy or becoming a writer? It is another question without an answer. Does it matter? If you're serious about writing you won't be wasting your time on addressing unanswerable questions in academic articles. At least, you won't be spending time on trying to get them into print any more than renowned philosophers would bother with storywriting competitions. Say what you want to say, and say it now!

The big Questions of Life can be answered differently for every person, real or fictional. The ideal way for writers to address difficult or sensitive subjects is through fiction. Here you are free to ask the question you want to ask, and can explore all the possible answers before finding the one that's right for you, or for your character, by the end.

Philosophy is thought to be a hard subject because it's full of jargon and is peppered with Latin words. Many eminent philosophers weren't very good writers because they couldn't put their ideas across to ordinary people - their academia got in the way.

Write Well

If fiction writing isn't your thing, you can still make good use of your gift with words, to make a real impact on the world.

> "I get so frustrated with people who can sit opposite me and tell me how painful their life is; and yet ask them to write it all down and they haven't a clue what to put," says someone who runs a self-help clinic.

Writers can do it and might consider helping others do it, because they can express the emotions that others can't define. If you take a visit to the emotions page you might find the words or examples you need for enriching the characters' lives in your fiction. Also try Get a Life! where we examine possible ways of better understanding human nature. If you cannot move millions through your writing, it is just as valuable to help even one person through the quagmire of their misery.

I strongly believe in making a piece of writing accessible to all. If you don't understand something whilst reading it carefully then dump it, because life is too short. Try again when you're a bit older.

I realise I'm putting my head on the block here but whatever you write, make sure the words are short, clear, accurate, and hang together in as accessible way as possible;

or you'll be dumped too. And perhaps never revisited.

Use Your Creative Energy

The urge to write raises itself especially over local and political issues. Short of sending out family newsletters to broadcast your opinions, writing to the local or national paper is an available and worthy outlet. These publications readily ask for your contributions so why not get your name known to the general public? Budding councillors and politicians seem to learn their trade in the local press. Budding writers can get themselves known that way, and get the buzz of publication: it's all part of the learning equation.

However, stop and think a moment. What chances might you be compromising by putting your thoughts into everyone's homes? Will it meet with approval from all directions if you openly express an opinion? What if it opposes that of your employers? Regardless of content, will future employers be keen to take on someone who speaks their mind loud enough for the dignitaries to hear? It could be an advantage - or the opposite.

You will be surprised at the fear that prevails in society. Writing is powerful and if you write very easily there may be some unexpected barriers standing in the way of what you want to do.

Is it right to clone human beings?

Should animals be killed for their fur?

Should Britain accommodate all asylum seekers?

Is it right to lower the age of consent for homosexuals?

What makes a terrorist?

We have some arguments to share and you may care to oppose them, or you might try using your writing as a tool of thought in exploring what you think on these subjects and others:

Psychotherapy is a Rip-Off

Publication is Unimportant

Artists Should Receive a Government Retainer

Stop all this Grown-up Parenting

Writing Horror Stories is Good for You

You don't have to know the history of philosophy to be able to ask 'unanswerable' questions and explore the answers in your own way. Fictional characters can become your servants: give them firm character traits and let them do the talking, the acting and the thinking. They'll give you an answer; they'll create a philosophy that's relevant to themselves.

You can hone your arguing skills in challenging the politics of the day, and you can easily wade in with your opinions, sending letters to the press, if you feel that way inclined. Involving yourself in politics will surely be a useful outlet for your writing. But I suggest you only do it if you think you can orchestrate and handle some immediate, if transient, fame or infamy. At author.co.uk we have an editorial page, known as Polemia, that can be used to express our outrage or to comment upon the issues of the day.

If privacy, imagination, deep and personal emotions are your motivation then novel writing (when it's published, even self-published) must be the most effective way to influence society.

Emotions

Writers are here to give words to the wordless. Playwrights, novelists, poets and songwriters put ideas and emotions into words where others cannot, or will not, say it. There's a song 'Everybody Hurts' that touches all who hear it - a wailing solo voice that makes you think 'yes, it's true. Everybody does hurt, sometimes'. Hitting on a truth in art is what matters.

Second only to music, emotions are our common denominator. Across the world we writers can empathise with the way other people feel, regardless of language and culture.

We learn emotions, far more easily than we learn plain facts. Emotions rub off on us from things we experience. Some are good - like love and faith; others are protective, like fear and disbelief; and still more are destructive, like hate and ennui.

Harness your emotions

The heartfelt pleas from jolted lovers, the anxious cries of deserted mothers, the lonely hearts of posted soldiers. The guilt-ridden angst of a palsied child's mother, the poverty stricken waif who knows of no future, the helpless family of adults with an ageing father. We need to understand, get messages understood, put emotions into writing because the written word gives power.

Personal experience is incredibly valuable to the writer. When you've written about an emotional encounter that shook you through and through, there'll be a bond of truth that you'll recognise; and you'll strive to capture it in everything you write.

If you can handle such strong emotions in writing, then fiction writing will come easily to you. And it will hit the reader where it matters.

Strong messages

Think about the feelings listed here. How can you show them without using the actual word? If the reader has to work it out, the stronger will be your message. This is your therapy, but it's put to good use. Take temporary ownership of any words below, stir them with empathy, add some complications like unfinished business or a rekindled grudge. Explore through fiction and make the world a better place.

    Happy
    Sad
    Love
    Hate
    Misery
    Jealousy
    Envy
    Regret
    Lust
    Suffering
    Angst
    Fear
    Motivated
    Ennui
    Pleasure
    Disgust
    Confusion
    Embarrassment
    Confidence
    Trepidation
    Excitement
    Astonishment
    Tired
    Faith
    Disbelief
    Satisfaction
    Frustration
    Humiliation

How do you show any of these emotions? Here is some fiction to get you thinking :-

Final Demand

I got blisters on my palms last time I went to see him. Well, it was me own fault really, I wanted to show off me new bike. Try it out, give it mileage.

I hadn't even meant to visit him but I was on my way up the slow old hill away from home, grinding my knee joints and jerking my head now and then with the effort, and I thought, once I get to the top I can go anywhere I please. And it pleased me to see him.

It pleased me to gush across the countryside, hedgerows pregnant with blossom buds, fresh new blades cleansing the stale flattened hay cushions of last year. Pillows, you could call the verges. Pillows tucked up against bramble-bordered duvets. Each field is an eiderdown of lumpy brown soil, soft enough to dive onto but scratchy enough to graze my temperamental skin.

Phew! It was hard work up that hill, and I felt hot inside big gloves but didn't think I'd get blisters. Had a look when I stopped at the village. I mean, you get blisters with new shoes, not a new bike.

Beside the gentle purr of my easy gears, the gravel popped and I scoured the road surface under the tyres. I swear I could hear my knees creak too. A pheasant shot out from a ditch as I passed, and its flight path christened the hedgerow with fear.

I stopped at the disused post office, to look at the postcards in the window. Sam hadn't retrieved his ad. Why had I bothered helping him to write it!

No newcomers were taking over yet. Blue oranges lay beside shrivelled apples, a few months' worth of free papers carpeted the doormat and I could just see an envelope addressed to him. Yes! Him!

That's what made me do it. I had an excuse to go and visit. See him. A kind of back-handed jibe. "It's no-one or me if you don't even pick up your mail."

I could tell him there was a letter 'care of' the village post office, and if he knocked up the person next door, they might be able to help. It looked personal: didn't look like a bill. "You can't be a hermit for ever. Aren't you curious?"

He answered the door. My legs felt like jelly. Oh no, not nerves - well I tell myself - it was from cycling for so long. I couldn't feel the blisters then, only sore. Hot and shaky, I was, from the effort.

He treated me like a princess, but without genuflecting. He didn't kiss my hand, didn't touch my arm, and didn't demonstrate our long strong bond in any way. He stood back, inviting me in, sort-of polite, careless, wordless. He's growing away, unlearning to love me, strangely distant: cancelling my vibes.

Before the bike ride out to see him I'd been pruning the roses. Last year's black spot was still evident on the few leaves. One or two petals were brown and shrivelled but most were quite gone, blown away. A single bud had failed to open and was still in one piece, the petals fused and brown.

I thought about us, then.

I cut the roses hard. I snipped the cuttings into finger-length twigs and put them in a paper sack. It waits in the shed, for burning in a fire. My fingers were still sore from the thorns as I cycled up the hill, pleased as punch with my new transport.

Now I can go see Sam anytime I want, if only he wanted.

My ultimatum had no real punch, I wonder why I bothered. He won't even open a letter from someone else. He pretends he wants no-one. I have to let sleeping dogs lie. A new bike, a new future. Wider horizons. Maybe the finger-pricks camouflaged the gradual chafing from my handlebar grips.

I didn't tell him, it would have stirred up old sores.

© Bernie Ross 2001

(You can see Anita's 'problem' that inspired this vignette on Get a Life!)

Strong Emotions

Do you understand how it feels to be adopted?

Different fictions 'work' for different people but I never really thought about an adopted child needing to find its natural mother until I watched Secrets and Lies, the film written and directed by Mike Leigh.

What is it like to lose a baby in cot death?

What are the dangers of malpractice in a factory near you?

Birth, marriage, death, divorce, imprisonment, injury, etc.. The major stress points of life are the obvious emotions worth exploring, but nothing is simple. Don't ignore the emotions that are trapped in your characters' blind spots (see Get a Life!) because your writing deserves to make the most of the opportunity - to touch your readers with real and believable truths.

It takes someone to write about an issue in a heartfelt way before it's taken seriously or a campaign is launched to make a change. Without writers who can articulate the strong feelings, the rest of us simply don't know.

Freedom Through Writing

When you've written about a deeply affecting experience of your own, it frees you to move on and away from it. You'll know how to capture the essence of truth in some other emotional issues because you'll know 'that special feeling' when you get there.

In Ellie's story 'Terminated', she deals with angst, anger, fear, sadness, frustration, acceptance, regret and more. Ellie is a forty-something novice writer, who lives in the Midlands with her partner and 2 daughters. Having recently trained as a counsellor, she decided not to pursue this avenue, although she is still fascinated by people and their relationships. She has handled these emotions so well, yet it is literary fiction. It hits on truth that women (and perhaps men) everywhere, will recognise.

I've never killed a man in real life but I've written it convincingly; and a whole lot of other emotional incidents too. And I plan to explore plenty more, and put them into words, to help others understand. If people can read something that makes them feel that they've 'been there' then maybe they will avoid the emotional pitfalls it revealed.

One Person, Only One

Within every enormous disaster there are individuals each with their own deep emotion. It is occasionally these personal accounts that bring home to us just how terrible a situation has been.

In the weeks following the terrorist attacks on the World Trade Centre in New York, we are able to read about the final phone calls, the frantic escapes, the horrific near-misses where - for a certain individual - it seemed as if a god was on their side. Without these personal stories we might just as well have been watching cartoons on the news. With the true, touching, personal stories we understand - and are all the more determined not to allow such atrocities to be worth instigating. It is more difficult to relate to the victims of other disasters or acts of terror when the individual stories cannot be told.

Handle emotions in writing; get to grips with the argument for or against, and - like some of the greats mentioned in Literary Clout - you'll be in a position to help change the world.

Terminated - by Ellie McLoughlin

5.50am. The luminescent figures of the alarm clock pierced the darkness. By this time tomorrow it will be over. An unreal, dreamlike quality pervaded her consciousness. She turned her head slowly, ensuring she barely moved the bedclothes. Deborah didn't want to wake him yet. She needed this final half hour to herself, alone with her thoughts. Once she got up, she'd be drawn into the process of getting ready.

The quiet stillness embraced her, calming her chattering mind. Gingerly moving her hands beneath the duvet, she rested them on her abdomen. She caressed her soft flesh, trying to detect some sign of movement, although she knew it was too soon. She turned her head to look at her sleeping husband. She'd thought she knew him so well, but was no longer sure. In the half-light his face looked serene and peaceful, as if his dreams were sweet and his conscience clear. How could he sleep at such a time, she wondered with a mixture of amazement and disgust.

As if he sensed someone watching him, Jonathan opened his eyes and looked at her. "What time is it?" he asked, stifling a yawn.

"Ten past six" she replied. "S'pose I might as well get up and get ready. I don't want to be late. You stay in bed a bit longer, if you like."

He positioned his hands behind his head and closed his eyes again. She noticed his beard was turning grey at the sides and slight pouches were developing beneath his eyes. An unexpected feeling of tenderness for him swept through her.

They hadn't talked about anything, other than

domestic trivia, since making their decision. Now a tension hung between them, palpable and heavy, the air thick with feelings neither of them dared to voice. As if by unspoken agreement, they'd ceased physical contact. Sighing, Deborah got out of bed and donned her peach housecoat and slippers. The new lilac satin dressing gown was packed ready in her overnight bag.

In the kitchen, Deborah felt the radiator. Still cold. She advanced the timer and the central heating clunked reluctantly into action. She poured herself a glass of water and placed it deliberately on the worktop. This was to be her sole sustenance for the immediate future. Her stomach growled, sounding like water regurgitating in a plughole. Of course, she was hungry for two now.

Out of habit, she filled the kettle and switched it on, making a mental note to descale it next week. No doubt, Jonathan would languish in bed, expecting her to take him a cup of tea. Usually she would do his bidding rather than risk the withering look of disapproval on his face.

She picked up her water and shuffled into the lounge. There, she set the glass on the coffee table and flopped onto the settee. She grabbed a purple cushion, wrapped her arms around it and buried her face in it. It was rough against her cheek and smelled faintly of fabric conditioner.

She'd never liked the week between Christmas and New Year. It was neither one thing nor the other, a kind of holiday limbo. The paper-chains hung tired and limp. Even the artificial Christmas tree appeared to be wilting. But it was too early to take them down. They had to keep up the façade, stop people becoming suspicious. What if someone visited unexpectedly? It would seem out of character if all their Christmas decorations had disappeared before New Year.

Deborah had gone through the ritual of family festivities in a daze, unable to absorb what was to happen. The world mocked her with its sudden abundance of pregnant women and babies. In the paper, on the television, in shops: she couldn't escape the cruel reminders of the joy she should be experiencing. She daren't let herself contemplate the possibilities or what ifs. In the queue in Tesco, two young women behind her had been discussing their morning sickness. She wanted to join in their conversation with her own experience, wanted to be a member of this nameless club that united countless women.

Jonathan was up. She could hear him moving about in the bathroom. That creaking floorboard gave him away. She sipped her water slowly, savouring its sharp coolness in her mouth. She looked at the clock, then at the photo next to it, on the mantelpiece. It showed Jonathan and his children. James and Anthony, the eight-year old twins, stood on each side of him grinning, and little Lucy, the apple of his eye, stood in front, with her father's hands resting on her shoulders. She remembered the day it was taken. She had been in bed with 'flu and Jonathan had taken the children to a safari park for the day. She flung the cushion down. "No point in putting off the inevitable" she mused aloud and went to get washed and dressed.

They arrived at the hospital at half past seven exactly. A young nurse, fresh-faced and oozing energy, showed them into a small white room off a long straight corridor of identical doors. She told

Deborah to get undressed and put on the white gown on the end of the bed.

The room looked cold and austere and was sparsely furnished. A heavy iron bed stood against one wall. The mattress was very high. Deborah had to stand on a small step to climb onto it. To one side of the bed were an armchair and a locker, to the other, an oxygen canister and several pieces of medical equipment laid out on a shiny steel trolley. She took off the clothes she'd only put on half an hour previously and pulled on the white regulation hospital gown. The fabric was cool and slightly stiff. She felt absurd, her small frame enveloped in so much billowing material, complete with full length split up the back. Jonathan said nothing except "I'll put your clothes in your overnight bag under the bed."

"Sure you want to go through with this?" Dr Forsythe asked as she ripped the sterile wrapper off the plastic tubing on the trolley beside her.

Deborah wavered. She studied Jonathan, sitting in dispassionate silence at the side of the bed. Whatever reassurance or reaction she had hoped for was not forthcoming. Jonathan fumbled in his pocket, withdrew a tissue and blew his nose. She'd turned the whole thing over repeatedly in her mind, since her pregnancy had been confirmed, before Christmas. Initially, Jonathan accused her of being devious, unable to believe that she hadn't realised sooner. Her periods had always been erratic.

Jonathan, who as he put it, knew her better than she knew herself, had eloquently and convincingly given her a list of reasons why this baby was out of the question. When they got married, he reminded her, it was with the understanding that there would be no children. He already had three, from his previous relationship and he did not want to be a father again. Jonathan's next point was that they couldn't afford a baby given their current financial position. Ok, so, they weren't well off, but neither were thousands of other couples who had children. They managed. Finally, he'd said, Deborah was in no fit state to look after a baby, what with her panic attacks. As usual, she couldn't fault his logic. She knew it made sense, but had hoped he might soften once he knew she was carrying their child.

Trapped, she had to choose between her husband and her baby. She wanted both. Losing her husband - the mere thought filled her with blind panic. And the thought of a baby, small, helpless and dependent on her… He was right; she would never cope. The underlying message, unspoken but insidiously implied, was that if she ignored his wishes and went ahead with the pregnancy, he didn't intend sticking around. Ultimately, she knew her loyalty had to be to her husband. Without him, nothing else mattered. And they had agreed to no children when they got married, so of course, she couldn't let him down now.

Deborah, apparently, was already about twelve weeks pregnant. Dr Forsythe, had talked to them about a termination and what it entailed at this later stage. A detailed description of what she would have to go through did nothing to lessen Jonathan's resolve. Ending the pregnancy was the only solution, he claimed, and Deborah like a good, compliant wife, agreed.

Dr Forsythe inserted the small tube between her thighs and into her cervix, explaining the procedure.

"This liquid prostaglandin will cause your cervix

to dilate and eventually you'll go into a sort of mini labour. It will be painful and protracted, but I've prescribed morphine for you for the pain. If you need a nurse, just press this buzzer." She placed a small plastic unit, with a rubber button on it, in Deborah's hand.

"I have to go now. Good luck," she said, patting her hand before leaving the room.

Terror seized Deborah and held on tight. She wasn't so sure about this now that she no longer had a choice. Inside she was crying, "no, no!" She wanted to tell someone she'd changed her mind, that she wanted her baby. But it was too late. Nothing could change the chain of events that she'd put into motion. They were hurtling towards an inevitable end like a runaway train. She was on a collision course of no return. Whatever happened, she would never hold this baby in her arms. The realisation was excruciating; she couldn't bear to think about it. With great willpower, she harnessed her mind to concentrate on her surroundings. The room looked unfriendly and clinical. The walls were painted pale green and the floor was covered with a green patterned lino. Easier to wipe the blood from, she thought. She looked at Jonathan, hoping for some distraction, if not comfort. He was leafing through the newspaper and chomping on a Mars bar.

"There should be a crossword in here somewhere," he said. "Fancy doing it with me?"

"Not at the moment". She couldn't comprehend how he could sit there eating chocolate as if he was at the cinema, while she was about to slowly and intentionally get rid of their baby. Her resentment stuck in her throat like dry toast that won't come up, but you can't swallow either. She'd always been unyielding in her belief that abortion was unacceptable under any circumstance. Until now, that is… Since discovering she was pregnant, she'd been unable to utter the word, "abortion" preferring "termination," which sounded less violent and destructive.

She awoke an hour later to a growing pain in her abdomen. It grew and grew in intensity, levelled out to a plateau and then slowly subsided. She bit her lip and clenched her fists tightly. Jonathan was now holding a book, but looking at her.

"How do you feel, Debs?" he asked.

"Rough. I'm getting bad pain now too. Has anyone been in while I was asleep?"

"No. Why don't you ask the nurse for an injection? The doctor said she'd prescribed morphine for the pain."

Deborah hesitated, "I'll probably be ok for a little while yet."

But as the pain increased in intensity and frequency, she realised she couldn't tolerate it. It took her breath away. It tore through her abdomen like no pain she'd ever experienced. In desperation, she pressed the little button in the palm of her hand. After several minutes, a fair-haired nurse wearing wire-rimmed glasses, poked her head around the door.

"Yes?" she said.

"Please… I'm in a lot of pain and Dr Forsythe said I could have an injection when it got too bad."

"Ok," responded the nurse. "I'll be with you when I can, but we're very busy. Lots of babies deciding to be born today, it would seem." As she closed the door, Deborah could hear a baby's plaintive cries seeping in from somewhere along the corridor.

She couldn't believe the brutality and insensitivity of putting her on the labour ward. Was it a punishment, she wondered, or a lesson designed to stop you repeating the situation? She had felt the nurse's frostiness in her pointed remark.

Ten minutes later, another nurse, older but no friendlier, came in bearing a kidney dish containing a hypodermic needle. She didn't smile or look Deborah in the eye, but told her to turn on her side and yanked her gown open at the split. Wordlessly, she stuck the needle into Deborah's buttock and the clear fluid coursed into her veins. She left the room as swiftly and quietly as she had entered. Deborah looked at Jonathan, tears welling up in her eyes. "It's not my imagination, is it? They're so cold towards me. It's because of the termination, isn't it?"

"No, no," he hesitated. "They're probably just very busy," he added, averting his gaze.

Within minutes, as the powerful drug began to surge through her body, Deborah felt light-headed and nauseous. The pain, while not having subsided, was now competing with these for her attention. She lay flat in an attempt to stop the bed swaying. Coloured spots and lights flashed before her eyes, but the pain was receding amid the firework display in her head.

The next time she looked at her watch, it was after two. She'd lost several hours to drugged sleep. When she rang the bell to ask for more morphine, she had to wait twenty minutes before anyone responded. She imagined they despised her and saw her as the lowest of the low. She envisaged them maligning her in their office over coffee. She could even sympathise with them. She wanted to tell them that she was anti-abortion herself. Yet, still she ached for someone to reach out, to hold her hand or stroke her hair.

The hours staggered by in a haze of pain and drug-induced stupefaction. Deborah tried to focus on her breathing, anything to divert her attention from the incessant, screaming pain tearing at her abdomen like a demonic beast. Throughout, she was aware of Jonathan's constant but silent vigil at her bedside.

Intermittently, she heard the wails of a newborn baby thrust unsuspecting, into the harsh light of reality. She wondered if she would ever be in that position herself. It was a privilege to bear a child and now that she had abused that honour, she felt that God would punish her accordingly. She was swamped by physical and emotional agony. She wished her life could end too. Glancing at her husband, she saw that he was once more engrossed in a book; oblivious to her torment. She turned to face the blank wall.

"You bastard" she thought. "Can I ever forgive you for making me choose? Why couldn't I have both? You and my baby. Most women do. Surely that's not being greedy."

Her outrage was overtaken by a new wave of pain that crashed over her unexpectedly, taking her breath from her and carrying her on its crest. She winced and grabbed the metal post at the head of the bed, holding it till the pain subsided.

After her next morphine injection, she drifted in and out of sleep between waves of agonising contractions. Her dreams were fragmented and surreal, merging aspects of real life with the bizarre.

When she awoke, Jonathan was standing at her bedside whispering her name.

"Debs, I'm going to go home for a bit and get some sleep. I'll be back later. You'll be okay?"

She couldn't tell if she was still dreaming, this was actually happening or she was hallucinating. She looked past him to the empty chair. He was going home, to bed, to sleep… while she was here going through her own private hell. It was true all right. He kissed her forehead and left the room. She felt desolate and childlike. She glanced back at the empty chair several times as if to reassure herself that she was alone.

When she woke again, an unfamiliar nurse was standing at her bedside, looking at her. The shifts must have changed while she was asleep.

"Are you all right?" asked the nurse. Her voice was soft and kind.

"Yes," Deborah replied, "but I think I need the loo."

"Hang on. I'll get you a bedpan. Oh, by the way, I'm Janice, your night nurse."

The nurse returned with a shiny steel bedpan and helped Deborah hoist herself up into a sitting position astride the bedpan. As she had been forbidden to drink all day, save an occasional sip of water, she was surprised at the urgency of her need to urinate. But she was beyond caring. She lolled back against the bed's metal headrest and relaxed her muscles, allowing the warm liquid to escape from between her legs.

Through the haze of morphine and exhaustion, she heard rather than felt, a dull plop in the pan. She struggled for consciousness like a drowning woman fighting to get her head above water. What had happened? Had she inadvertently opened her bowels? Before she could guide her thoughts through the sludge of her mind, the nurse reappeared and gently pulled the bedpan from under her. When she saw the contents of the bowl, her face darkened and she hurried out of the room without a word.

Janice returned moments later and standing at the side of Deborah's bed, she picked up her hand and gently squeezed it.

"That's it," she said. "It's all over."

It took several minutes before the meaning of Janice's words sunk in. Deborah placed her hands on her abdomen and looked up at the ceiling. She swallowed the lump in her throat, which threatened to choke her. She'd chosen Jonathan, but now when she needed him most, he wasn't here. She'd given up a child for him and yet where was he in her hour of need. "Has my husband phoned?" she asked, mentally willing Janice to say what she wanted to hear.

"No love, he hasn't. But I'm sure he'll be back soon. The doctor will be here shortly to check you over."

"Can I go home then?" asked Deborah. "I want to go home. I want to go home tonight."

"No dear, they'll keep you in overnight just to make sure everything's all right and then you can go home in the morning. It's nearly eleven o'clock, you know."

The doctor was young, good-looking and looked as if he'd had too little sleep. He checked her thoroughly internally and asked how she felt. She couldn't answer that question, as she honestly had no idea. Her feelings, like her husband, seemed to have abandoned her. Jonathan hadn't returned and she imagined him at home, tucked up in bed, sleeping soundly.

When the doctor had given her the once over, Janice returned with a bowl of warm, soapy water and a yellow flannel and towel. "Come on, love," she said, helping her sit up. "Let's freshen you up a bit, eh? Then someone will wheel you over to the ward, you can get some sleep and go home tomorrow."

Janice washed Deborah's face and hands with exaggerated gentleness. She was touched by her tenderness, which was in such contrast to her previous treatment that day. She still yearned for someone to hold her, stroke her hair and tell her that everything would be fine.

Later, a porter wheeled her bed across the tarmac of the car park and in through the swing doors of the main hospital building. The sky was dark but clear.

"Blimey. There's a bit of a nip in the air tonight," he said. "Reckon we're in for a right old frost."

Deborah mumbled her agreement, preferring not to engage in conversation with this man she didn't know. She wondered if he knew that she'd had an abortion.

She felt self-conscious, as if everyone knew, as if she had a discerning mark that told people what she'd done. Realising that she didn't want to make small talk, the porter whistled instead. She recognised the tune, but couldn't put a name to it. It was one of those irritating commercial pop songs. The kind they played repetitively on certain radio stations. If someone told you the title and asked you to hum it, you'd never remember it. But if you heard it play in the morning, it would stick in your head for the rest of the day, no matter how hard you tried to get rid of it.

In the lift, she closed her eyes and concentrated on trying to remember the name of the song as the porter continued to whistle. He wheeled her down a darkened corridor and into a small dimly lit room, which contained three empty beds. He parked her bed in the space where a fourth had previously stood.

"There we go," he said.

"Thanks," Deborah muttered grudgingly.

"I'll tell Sister you're here."

Deborah turned on her side and drew her legs up to her chest. She wrapped her arms tightly around her knees and lay in the dark, her eyes wide open, watching and listening.

She wondered whether Jonathan was on his way back yet and if he was, whether he'd be able to find her. She wanted to warn someone that he might be looking for her, but she wasn't sure she could stand up yet, let alone walk. Suddenly aware of a whispered rustling from the sheets, she realised she was rocking herself, slowly, almost imperceptibly. It was a habit from childhood, used to soothe herself when she'd been sent to her room for some misdemeanour or other.

A cry startled her. Even to her inexperienced ear, she recognised a new-born baby. She turned onto her other side facing the doorway, which gave a clear view of the corridor. A woman scuffed past, a small bundle in her arms. She appeared mesmerised by whatever she was holding. Another howl pierced the quiet. Deborah understood now. She was on the maternity ward, with women who had recently given birth.

As she listened to another cry emanating from along the corridor, she could no longer hold back. Hot tears coursed down her cheeks, stinging the skin in their pathway. As she gave in, deep sobs convulsed her body. She cried for her baby, lost forever to this world, but most of all she cried for herself, trapped and alone amongst women who had their babies in cots beside them. Was her baby a girl or a boy, she wanted to know? What had the nurse done with it after she'd left the room? Was it recognisable? These questions and more flooded her mind, but there was nobody there to answer them.

She must get some sleep. Jonathan would be there to collect her the next morning and she didn't want him to see her with red, swollen eyes. She wriggled down in the bed and pulled the covers over her head. It was over now and time to put it behind her. There was no reason to mention the events of today ever again. They could pick up where they'd left off and pretend it had never happened. Slipping into sleep, she wondered if they could do something special for New Year…

Terminated © Ellie McLoughlin 2001

Argue - and Trigger Debate

Every writer needs an outlet for theories, complaints and philosophising. There are numerous sites on the World Wide Web that can accommodate your voice. Of course, you have to find your voice first. Decide where you stand on an issue, or make an issue over something that matters to you, by exploring it through writing.

Arguments to Stand your Hair on End

Do these rants and think-pieces make you write in reply? I hope so.

While I think it's important to be alert to world affairs, I don't particularly advocate spending time reading - or writing for - political activism. It plays havoc with your time and it suffocates your imagination. However, if you feel strongly about something I think you should write it, even if it only ever remains hidden in a drawer or on your PC.

You can try pasting your articles and 'rants' on web sites like www.writtenbyme.com, where there's the chance for feedback from other individuals, anywhere in the world.

As an alternative to the general 'paste your rant here' sites, your favourite campaigning organisation might be glad to host your having your say. At author.co.uk/polemia we allow ourselves the luxury of free speech that rarely brooks debate.

Do some of these think-pieces deserve debate?

Psychotherapy is a Rip-Off

If you have misery, learn to live well on it. I certainly intend to make the most of mine.

In the past ten years or so Counselling Therapy has become the vogue. Fairly recently I got caught up in watching a TV discussion programme about the pros and cons of this fashionable 'treatment'. As usual with these forums there was a lot of sense spoken, and challenged by opinions from a good many sentimental and even crackpot speakers. One voice stayed with me though. It was a middle aged professional woman who works in health. She made her point in words to the effect of the following.

"Everyone needs to talk things over and some of us have experienced really bad times. Done things we regret." She was right there, and you can't just talk about it to any odd stranger. She went on: "There isn't a network of family support for some of us, or perhaps we NEED a stranger who's far removed."

Yes. That's why the queue gets so long in the doctor's, or even the supermarket.

"We need someone who has a hard shell to weather some of the painful telling."

Correct, I thought.

"I have to admit," said the woman, "that I went for counselling some time ago. The first few sessions were good for unloading, and with some positive in-put I felt I came to terms with things. Nevertheless, my counsellor told me I still had a complex set of problems to explore, which really required many more sessions - all at a price, of course. I agreed to further sessions. However, this seemed to be the case repeatedly. In the end I decided to draw a line under it. I'd shared my troubles: now I would look to the future."

Well I'm glad she said those things and I hope it helped many other people think it through the way I have.

I'm a trained counsellor but I use what I've learned for my writing. Above all, I use my knowledge of psychology for writing characters in fiction and drama. Empathy is essential in fiction writing. My training is also inevitably helpful in empathising with troubled students.

I've met people who have had unhelpful brushes with counselling therapy, and it always seems to involve paid consultants in the private sector. In Britain, the National Health Service provides limited courses of therapy through their doctors' referral, and it can be very hard to get when you need it.

Personally, I think counselling should only be available in this way. As a creative writing tutor I'm aware that I could constantly tell people their work isn't yet good enough, that it needs this and needs that. On those grounds my 'income' could be almost guaranteed for life; but that's not my way.

Similarly the work of the private therapeutic counsellor could be tainted with an ulterior motive: to keep clients paying the money - a self-perpetuating affair.

Television audiences are notoriously vociferous about their problems, that's why they're there. The studio is an exciting rostrum, and - like the therapist's presence - it also provides a safety net. Deep seated and unspoken disturbances need a carefully managed strategy, which is overseen or contained by a neutral, independent professional. But do such programmes ever reach any truth? Or are they just entertainment?

I encourage writers - my students - to go on writing without my prompts, through writers' groups and by submitting to competitions, publishers and editors. Like Trevor (he says), I will never be rich because I'm too honest.

I wouldn't wish to accuse private therapists of any

dishonesty but it must be possible to unwittingly perpetuate clients' ongoing misery. The risk to the client is greater.

With writing you accumulate a body of work to show for your efforts. With counselling you may only end up with a confused, screwed up mind.

Useful books:
'Be Your Own Counsellor' by Sheila Dainow
'Self-Discovery Through Creative Writing' a Writing Life publication
'How to Survive Without Psychotherapy' by David Smail

Publication is Unimportant

Now that I've established myself in the vocation of my choice, I don't want to give any time to socialising in a way that will divert my diligence from my life's work.

On receiving an invitation to meet up with past colleagues, for old-times' sake, I sent my apologies with a refusal. My time is too precious at the moment to share it with people for the sake of indulgence.

Time is too short to be committing myself to occasions I don't really want. Time is running out for all of us. The years flit past quickly when you're over 25 and they call it 'over the hill' because you gather up speed, with the time going faster and faster.

Thinking along these lines I'm realising that I must get on and finish the various things I'm writing, and pursue the ideas I've got floating around in my head, to make something good of them. I want to explore the projects I know I could achieve. I must do these things to ensure there's something to show for the 49 years of my life: there could be so few of them left.

With age and experience the phrase "something to show for it" transcends all boundaries of physical or visual properties. That "something" might be someone's smile, someone's memory, someone's change of mind. Writing is the creative vehicle I use.

The fact that I express myself through writing, where others may do so through painting, making things, singing, mending, caring for the sick et al, means I'm lucky. It is possible that my view on the world can be accessible for many generations to come. It will not have to decay and become irreparable, and if forgotten then it can be revived simply enough.

Writing is what I do and by sharing it there is a faint hope that my ideas and my empathy will meet up with a thought receptacle in another person, and do them some good. Perhaps it will even snowball to do a lot of good for a lot of people. But if nobody reads it, I need not fret, for even the fact that I've written it will have enabled me to speak about the thought and therefore influence the listener. My notes and my manuscripts will exist after my death, but even if they don't, writing used as a tool of thought is good enough reason to do it.

A letter, a discussion, notes in a book, a play, a film, an advert, et al - all can change someone's life if it's right for them to receive it at a crucial, relevant moment. It is unimportant to be published. By sharing my ongoing work, through reading at a group, performing, lending or submitting manuscripts, my writing is reaching others' minds.

Getting published is good too. My thoughts might reach more people and so have more chance of meeting with the right receptacle at the right time. And if it pays - well, it allows further thoughts to be written instead of being lost in a quagmire of employment-related anxieties.

I write to share thoughts, ideas and wisdom, as well as to put order into the chaos of my mind. I think everyone should write and if they did then society would be wiser and more innovative. If only they would all use their brains! We must find our own balance between reading and writing, and forge ahead as best we can.

Striving to get published and writing for a specific market with the sole purpose of payment is detrimental to the writer. This thinker, this leader of thought needs to say whatever is in his head, for it is that which will meet with the mind of the reader.

The true, honest, pourings from the heart make for writing that matters. Writing for publication and pay, you see therefore, is irrelevant.

Artists Should Receive a Government Retainer

An artist is an artist, and the need for every person's self-expression will be fed through all forms of art. The population must reflect itself through writing, through painting, photography, sculpture, pottery, performance et al if it is to reach its full potential in civilisation.

The artist needs to eat and be warm, be loved, emotionally supported and supplied with an ongoing abundance of physical and mental material - he therefore needs to be paid a subsistence allowance for his artist life.

To be paid for his art products is the next best thing to receiving a retainer, but it isn't ideal because it will influence the output. A subsistence allowance will offer freedom to create, and it must cover essentials plus a little more.

The money must cancel out the need to turn out pretty paintings or soppy stories even though they do pay more than innovative new work. The tendency for people is to go on reaching for the better money at the expense of experimental art. But at the coal face of experimental art is where we should be! Touching boundaries, pushing a step further than the last person dared to reach.

An artist's role is to reflect society, stand back from it and help the rest of us to do so: see life and behaviour for what it is.

An abundance of pretty paintings and formulaic stories do not reflect the real world, they do not show much of the truth. Society - by paying for only the pretty or sensational sights - is misusing and abusing the artist.

Society that doesn't recognise the artist is like a man applying a blindfold and then saying it's not his fault for being unable to see. The allowance must be small but enough, and independent. It shouldn't be means-tested.

In striving for payment an artist will seek desperately for inspiration. It is this scraping of the barrel which often brings out the best!

So feed us, clothe us, stop us having to take distracting and time-consuming employment simply to keep ourselves alive. Leave us to get on with creating unpopular, groundbreaking, artwork. Our want and need to do it are so great. Nobody else can or will.

Stop all this Grown-up Parenting

I have seen the infamous girl in town: a 14 year old chubby person with a baby of her own, she was pushing its pram. Mother and child are here, thousands of miles away from the child's dad.

She met him on holiday in the Far East, became pregnant, and married him there and then. Aged 13, and with her parents consent. When the tabloid newspapers heard of it they came to life like a chicken shed ignited by fire.

When I saw the girl I wanted to speak to her, as she pushed

the pram past, head wrapped in a scarf like her Turkish in-laws. I didn't, I was shy: she might be fed up with comments, strangers stopping, or whisperings behind her back. Who knows what sharp tongues people have used against her?

Perhaps I have something different to say. I shall not criticise. I want to congratulate her on having her baby and I want her to know what a good thing she may have done to have started a family so young. When she can get back to her husband and start a proper life with him I wish them both the very best of luck and love.

I get so cross about test-tube babies and people demanding their rights to have a child by scientific methods under the NHS. They expect to do it at the expense of people who need hospital care through no fault of their own: illness through natural complications.

The time to give birth is when you're young, and I would say that, wouldn't I. I was a mother at 18. I will not say it was easy, nor do I expect she has found it easy, but then I doubt if any parent would wholeheartedly say that having a baby to look after is easy. Especially when there seems to be only one of you to bond with the child.

Perhaps this girl has been luckier than I. Her parents have been backing her, all the way. Their motives have been questioned but I wonder if they've had time to think in depth about the philanthropic issue.

People have become selfish and warped in the past 20 years. They regard it as their right to buy and own a house, and their right to work to that ambition. Well that's fine. Then they get to their late 20s, or mid-30s and start to think about having a baby, but it doesn't happen straight away. For some it doesn't happen at all. For those who do have children they regard it as their right to choose to put it in nursery, or - at least - they say it's essential but of course it isn't. They choose to pay the highest possible mortgage: to ensure there is a roof over the family's heads.

And the children's childhood is shaped.

Oh, there are toys galore, activities and plenty of love from the nursery staff, but the children aren't learning how to cope with the boredom of finding things to play with at home. They're not learning much about home life, they're learning how to manipulate events to fit into convenient pockets. And when no one can be 'in-charge' properly (while equipment is moved, activities prepared) they might be consigned to passively watching TV.

There is one way the Government made a huge, unsightly mistake in shaping our society. It was the decision - in the early '80s - to allow couples to take out a mortgage on the basis of both their salaries, instead of only one.

People thought that in just 3 or 5 years their payments would be low enough, single salary high enough, or property escalated in value enough, for the wife to give up her job to have a child. Not so.

The 'giving up' became 'maternity leave' only, so then the child had to be farmed out. That's if the wife managed to conceive.

As a woman gets older, she becomes less fertile, and if a couple plan to have a family when the wife is in her 30s, the dream may be impossible to fulfil. Only after years of trying and consequent tests do they realise there's a problem and that IVF or other treatment has to be sought. Their greed for home-ownership and having a life before children puts paid to the reward they'd always envisaged for their mutual love. They seek that pay-off through scientific means and at the indisputable invalids' cost.

So I want to say to this girl with the pram, under her headscarf, "Enjoy your motherhood, young mum. Play with your child as if you never grew up. Use the wisdom - that your responsibilities have thrust upon you - to make a worthwhile experience for you both. It may have been only 10 years since you poured water on your toys in the bath, or built towers with brightly coloured bricks in the back yard, but let these fresh memories be an asset to your skills. Play with your child like a sibling."

There aren't enough parents who are wise enough to allow themselves to be young enough to play with their children on equal, childish terms.

Most people are too busy trying to be grown up to be able to give their children what they really need. "So listen, young mum. You - in your fame - can show the world you were right."

Society will be more content, and younger; if only parents would stop being so horribly grown up.

A Different Perspective

I worry that the world is watering down its skills and intelligence. Where is Darwinism in all this social concern? How will Homo sapiens move ionwards towards Homo electronicus if no effort is made to increase our intelligence? Surely we would be better off destroying every male child. That may bring some peace to a fractured and unequal world?

Columnists and sketch writers abound taking prime space in newspapers and magazines. They often provide a biased viewpoint and some revered voices continue when they are clearly bereft of any new ideas. One national newspaper has allowed one of their columnists to moan on about her ex-husband interminably. Clearly the paper has good reasons for allowing such twaddle to continue but it does suggest that writers must always read everything with a critical eye. The Polemia column at author.co.uk rumbles along and occasionally faces castigation but it has a firm base. Whether I am right or wrong, and only history will tell, I believe in my writing at the time it is written. My brain can't spring forward to provide any defence in the future. I may be able to provide some answer immediately after the articles are posted but why should I have to do so? I write the words, I display them on a web site free of charge. The reader must make of them what they will. Once they have left my brain they must stand alone for I have no wish to turn over detritus.

Writing Horror Stories is Good for You

There are very good reasons for writing horror stories, and it isn't only because it sells well.

Yes, people like to glean atrocities, and our newspapers sometimes seem to wallow in their disgusting proof. Appealing to the voyeur in us all is a good enough reason for some, but there is more to it: Writing and reading horror is a good, life enhancing experience.

Writers need to do it as part of their learning to write really well: as an education in handling sensitive and taboo subjects. What that entails is up to the individual. The exercise of writing horror can remain personal and doesn't have to be published; for the act of doing it will benefit the writer.

In many cases the horror shouldn't be published unless it's a fine piece of literature. Horror is worse than nauseous if it has been badly written. No, there are greater and more profound reasons for writing and publishing horror stories, both true and fictional.

Civilization thrives on reproduction, and reproduction in itself thrives on two things: sexual appetite, and attachment. We are born attached to our mother and we bond with our nearest and dearest in varying degrees as we grow. We take these things for granted, and because we do, we inevitably ignore the bonding.

We abuse the right to have these attachments, by rebelling, or hurting the ones we love most; all in the cause of being our own person. For example, we coldly separate ourselves from parental protection when we rebel as teenagers or when we leave home for good. Sometimes these life changes have to come about in a callous way simply in order to achieve the independence we require. Stupidity might reign, but stupidity is a subjective thing.

Separation comes about in numerous ways, both emotionally and physically, and it is usually harder for one party than the other, though occasionally both. Separation triggers a sadness and grief which in turn fuels a yearning for re-attachment: a desire for a love connection to be fully and unconditionally established.

"Absence makes the heart grow stronger." It is not until we're forced apart that we realise the bond that existed.

Because of this innate need for each of us to belong to someone, to be emotionally attached to another human, we are all aware of the sadness experienced when connection fails. The one inevitable event in every life is death itself. Sadness is therefore a common denominator.

Many people will say they've never experienced true love, but how many can say they've never experienced loss, grief or sadness? Sooner or later we are subjected to losing someone through death.

Sadness becomes something by which we can measure the other emotions in our lives: notably love. Sadness makes us appreciate love and its unconditional attachment. Without sadness we cannot measure the strength of our feelings in the other areas of life that matter.

Reading horror stories, where atrocious actions and taboo emotions are explored carefully and sensitively through the written word, helps us all to establish, to justify for ourselves, or realign our own emotional dispositions.

As a child you have to do something naughty at least once, to test yourself or your carers: to discover the true boundaries of their discipline.

As an adolescent you have to career off course - go wayward - if only briefly before growing out of it. Writing horror (and erotica) is like another milestone in development. They are all vital steps that are necessary to you, as a writer, to move forward.

Writing horror and other taboo material is good for the writer because it sharpens the skill of combining observation and imagination in a collection of detailed, sensitively handled words. These words will move the reader to a new and better-equipped emotional disposition. This is the crux: seeing and reading gratuitous sex and violence is harmful and distasteful, but if the work offers understanding of the perpetrator and the vulnerability of the victim, then it makes opportunities for healing and prevention.

Reading horror stories - in moderation and well written of course - are therefore an essential constituent in a diet of good literature.

Why else would The Bible have been such permanent reading, a basis for so many literary and dramatic achievements, and such a best seller for so long?

Want an argument?

Write a reply to one of the above. Send it to argue@author.co.uk

Look at the 10 commandments - when is there a case for breaking one of them?

Look at your other religious 'bibles' and write an argument for, or against.

Explore any of the following concepts or their web sites, using them as starting points and more:

Peace and anti-war issues:

• The Centre for War and Peace Studies www.cwps.org

• For mother earth www.motherearth.org

• Disarmament links www.igc.apc.org

• Nobel Peace Prize Archives: www.almaz.com/nobel

• War Resisters International: www.netaxs.com/

• Conscientious objectors: www.objector.org

• Peace News: www.gn.apc.org/peacenews/

• Peacewire: www.peacewire.org

Section Three

The Wider World

We move on from the craft of writing to a wider world. Much that has been discussed so far applies to all writing, not just writing fiction. Putting together any collection of words is a creative process. In so doing you are producing literature.

Most writers need someone to read their work. It has become accepted practice that the writers shall write, and then pass those words to someone else to publish. It was not always like that and today there is no real need for it to be that way. Finding a publisher certainly takes a weight from the writer's shoulders. However there may be drawbacks. Whether you use a publisher or some other pathway you, as a writer, must take responsibility for your work.

This section will present a number of possible pathways that allow the writer to reach an audience. It is not comprehensive but like all of the material in this book and its associated CD-ROM it can do no more than stir your imagination, make you consider the appropriate action for you.

Read Your Work

What could be easier? Read your work to a friend, relative or a local group of people or just to yourself. It will ensure the words flow smoothly and provide some measure of your potential. Those writing for children can rely upon a critically honest audience as a child will tell you the truth. Adult reactions can be more subtle but still identifiable. Join a writers' circle as that will give you an invaluable platform.

Record Your Work

It is relatively simple to record your work on to an audiotape in your own home. The quality may not be perfect but it is another useful tool that can be used to send to distant friends or as a promotional tool. There is a Spoken Word Association, an amalgam of writers, actors and producers who work together to make audiotapes. These tapes and CD's are one of the biggest growth areas for writers, and should not be ignored. A tape of commercial quality will need to be professionally produced but there are a surprising number of sound studios that can be hired for a few hours and resting actors are always delighted to help.

Writers' Circles

A question frequently asked of author.co.uk is "How do I find other writers in my area?" The support of a writers' group is vital to those writers who find it difficult to write in isolation. My own writers' group Felixstowe Scribblers is small, and none of us can be described as successful authors. Some of the members have had articles published, and there is the occasional published writer with a real book on their shelves but most members just enjoy writing. Less than a dozen people attend meetings regularly although nearly forty people have attended more than once during the last two years. It is the small size and fluidity of the group that aids its vitality. There is no formal structure and we are lucky as the excellent Suffolk County library service allow the group to use the local library for evening meetings.

Writers' circles vary in their approach. Some groups exist to serve only professional writers or particular interest groups; perhaps poetry or play-writing. There are postal workshops and email discussion groups which can draw their members from anywhere in the world. Look at the sites such as www.yahoo.co.uk, www.topica.com and www.lyris.com who organise mailing lists and search there for groups for writers.

Finding a Group

Finding a group should be fairly easy. There is a list of the groups on the author.co.uk site. It is not comprehensive, as it is virtually impossible to produce a definitive guide but the contacts listed, even if they do not cover your own area may be able to help. Telephone or email the contact name of a group that is fairly close to where you live, and ask their advice. Writers are usually socially aware and if they don't know of a group near you they will probably know of someone who can help.

Another good place to start looking is the local library as they often have a list of local groups and associations. Most groups meet at least once a month, often in a local hall or in members' homes.

The writing class at the adult education centre or other local college can also be a useful point of contact. If no group exists in your area perhaps your classmates would be interested in starting a group. Often good teachers will encourage students to set up groups for mutual support, and may well attend and organise the initial meetings. Some professional tutors run training sessions in creative writing that are called writers' circles. That may be stretching the definition slightly but you pay the money, so the choice is yours. These can be very useful if the tutor concentrates upon the processes of writing and acts as mentor and support.

The local Arts Council will be able to assist so talk to the Literature Officer who is invariably a great source of information. Most local councils have an arts advisory service of some kind, and once again the stalwarts running these departments may be able to help, putting you in touch with local contacts and they often produce a newsletter for arts and/or literary interest. Many of these workers may be members of the National Association for Literary Development www.nald.org.uk

If despite all these contacts you still cannot trace other

local writers an article (keep it short) to your local newspaper may produce results, and the libraries will probably have a local groups display area. Approach the staff at the local bookshops; get them interested in your project as well. They may offer discounts to members of your group, and there are many good reasons to combine writing with reading. Don't forget those boards in newsagents' windows, supermarkets and other large warehouse stores as many people read them.

Group Structure

The structure adopted by individual groups varies considerably. Many have a formal constitution with officers elected annually and membership fees. This administration imposes an additional burden upon the hapless office holders but is often required if public halls are to be hired or the group plans to publish its own work. Such a structure can also be worthwhile if the group wishes to apply for grants or the support of local business, as it tends to inspire some confidence in the stability and integrity of the group.

Other groups, and mine is one, prefer to adopt a more casual approach. A group leader is necessary or one of the group members needs to be willing to use their address, telephone and email as a point of contact but beyond that there is freedom. This can work very well if the group is relatively small and has a reliable leader or small cohesive team that can continue to co-operate and meet regularly without dispute.

Whatever structure is determined the group will soon create its own social dynamic. Be aware that too often valuable associations are destroyed by the egoism of one or more members of the group who use meetings for self-aggrandisement. These ego-trips can be minimised if meetings follow an agreed timetable, one that ensures that every member in turn has the opportunity to personally address the meeting. Ideally each member should be asked to read something at each meeting. It is not sufficient to say that anyone is free to speak at any time, as many writers are shy and retiring and can be overshadowed by dominant personalities.

What Do They Do?

Some groups exist only to bring together writers to be addressed by speakers, usually well-known writers or other experts drawn from the world of writing and publishing. In such groups providing a personal platform may not be so important but an occasional meeting that enables members to read and present some of their own work can be invaluable.

The meeting provides an opportunity to present your writing to a wider world, especially to a group of fellow-writers, which often makes a writers' circle so appealing. Tapping away at a computer in the isolation of a spare bedroom is a lonely experience. Getting out into the wider world, gaining information about the latest competitions and events, sharing experiences with friends and, most importantly, reading your work to a small group can be very rewarding. The reaction of those who have listened to your reading can be interesting. This is another area that needs careful handling, as criticism can be very hurtful and very discouraging. It may be better not to allow much more that the most cursory of judgements during a meeting. Consider creating an email discussion list that will allow more considered discussion than is possible during a meeting.

Scribblers Do It This Way

Each group will organise its meetings differently, and this is not the place to do more than make some suggestions. Describing a meeting of my own group at Felixstowe may help. We meet fortnightly on a Tuesday evening at 7.30 pm. Our leader, Dave Feakes, starts with announcements; apologies for absence and items of news, as the advertising flyers he has received since the last meeting are passed round.

Group leaders will soon begin to receive information about competitions, events, new books and speakers willing to address the group may approach the leader and there will be advertisements for strange equipment - much of this will be of interest to someone in the group. There will also be more promises from vanity publishers - all of which should be culled by the leader.

In our group that early discussion is free-flowing, led by Dave, but with everyone joining in, often adding snippets of news unrelated to the business of writing, but which do help increase the cohesiveness of the group. Members of the group become friends, even though we come from totally different backgrounds and may not choose to meet socially. This interchange and chit-chat is an invaluable part of the meeting. This process may take 10-15 minutes.

Each member of our group is normally expected to produce material for each meeting, and to read their work to the group. Often this is based upon a word or short phrase, recent choices have been; 'transport', 'arrest or a rest', 'the sea' with one popular choice being 'lust', which provided interesting insights into members' characters and made for a very jovial meeting. Incidentally the most popular story produced at that meeting was about a group of small schoolchildren who having discovered this new 'rude' word began an investigation to discover what it really meant. It is helpful to take several copies of your work to the meeting, so enabling others to read the written word as you speak. We have at least one member who is hard of hearing who is grateful for a written copy. Alternatively pieces are often posted to the email list or even on the Web site, inviting considered judgements later.

Having a Read

Each member of the group will read their work in turn, normally lasting no more than five minutes. Group leaders may find they need to curb the time allotted to individuals, or some people will take advantage and plough on interminably. The next stage is where most conflict can arise. My group tends to make enthusiastic or very supportive comments following the reading, only rarely will a particular piece of work be criticised. Perhaps we are all too polite, and so miss out on receiving constructive, if harsh, comments but our approach seems to work well. Too often the criticism that can erupt after a reading in some groups is heavily loaded with extraneous purpose and it can be counter-productive. If criticism is to be encouraged it is probably better to set aside a session for that purpose with members commenting upon work that they have some time to consider. It is more productive to encourage comments from several people rather than to rely upon the pronouncements of the group sage, who may be dismissive of work that challenges their own authority or does not conform to a particular vision of 'good' writing.

The next part of our meeting is a discussion of the readings. This may not last very long, but there is no doubt that the obligation to produce work, perhaps even the competitive element of writing around a given theme does produce results. Our leader is a wise old owl preferring to allow a weak piece of work to pass uncommented, but later he will introduce discussion about plot or sentence construction, or use of tenses or genre - or whatever else may have been revealed during the reading sessions.

As we normally have continuing projects the meeting will end with a progress report. As I write we are starting a playscript and considering production of an anthology. These are dealt with outside of the general meeting, increasingly using our own mailing list, created using www.topica.com. Our man Dave always writes an account of the meeting to keep all members informed, particularly those who cannot attend the meetings through illness, disability or just other commitments. This mailing list and the group website support the regular newsletter which is distributed locally, and help to keep this writers' circle involved with its local community.

It can be argued that this approach will not help the novelist struggling with structure, the poet with lyrical form or the dramatist create better situation. That is not the purpose of this description, it is just to point out what works for our group, serving the needs of our majority quite well. Nothing is perfect and the actions of my group are not presented as an exemplar merely as an indication that some purpose, structure and intended outcomes need to be considered.

Maintenance of a group requires constant vigilance. There will be continual decay as people drift away, for any number of reasons. The group leader should try to discover why folk are leaving - it may be something within the group that needs to be changed. A regular press release will keep the group's activities in the public domain and endear local journalists but do keep it succinct and pertinent. Send out a press release whenever an interesting event occurs within the group. A public statement is required whenever a member wins a competition, finds a publisher or publishes a book, or if a successful local author addresses the group.

Increasingly writers groups are producing their own work. This may be a simple booklet or a more ambitious anthology could use our own print on demand service.

A writers' circle is an invaluable element within our society. It brings together erudite and intelligent people who invariably can make valuable contributions to the local community. Individual group members gain succour and information from the group, and the local society gains as the writers' circle collates the efforts of its writers. All writers should join a local group, however experienced they may be it will always be worthwhile.

Using the Internet

This is a fast-moving world whose users are well-served by instructional Web sites and books. Our advice is to spend as much time as you can to understand how all the systems that make up the Internet work. It will not be time wasted.

The Internet is part of the digital world that is expanding to include very many different devices. The Internet is a collection of systems, the World Wide Web (WWW) and email are the two most widely used. Slowly these systems are being integrated and information can now be created in one basic format that then allows it to be displayed on a Web TV, a mobile phone, in electronic books (ebooks) and many other places, including streaming news on the radio and on a variety of multi-media devices. Commercial companies initially saw the Internet as a gold-mine but have slowly realised that the public demand more than hype. In the search for ways to realise the possibilities presented by the Net large companies are slowly learning lessons.

Content Providers

Internet users want Web sites that provide useful content, at no cost at the point of supply. For companies selling simple products that poses a problem. Once you've glanced at the chocolate bar, fizzy drink or hamburger - what then? To overcome the basic weakness of many businesses; that they sell a very simple product many sites now provide 'content' (the new name for interesting words) and some are using writers to provide the material that will encourage return visits to sites. Unfortunately a few Web sites are asking writers for content but are not paying for the product. A variety of excuses are being provided. Writers are urged to post articles to sites that will be offered for sale to editors and publishers. When a sale is made the writer will be paid and the writer will gain invaluable exposure from display at such a prestigious site. There are a number of variations upon this theme, with some sites paying a 'click-through' commission every time a user leaves the writer's page to go to (click-through) an advertiser's site. Or commissions will only be paid when a user buys something from the advertiser's pages.

Honest and honourable people run most of these Web sites although there are always crooks hiding beneath the cloak. Whatever variety is used the real worry is for the individual writer as it is highly unlikely they will gain much from the exercise. A site may contain thousands of pages and so be a very attractive place to visit. The writer who has just one page among these thousands enters a lottery. Their work must first be selected from many, and then the user has to react in a pre-determined fashion before the writer will gain any commission. It may get worse as the commission may not be payable until a minimum sum has been reached, perhaps £100.

The site owners gain from these schemes for they receive small bites from many cherries. The cheery writer willingly supplying hard-wrung words upon a promise is often left disenchanted.

Warnings

Throughout this book there are warnings for the writer. They are not meant to discourage but writers are often so desperate to see their work published that caution is thrown to the wind. Be wary, particularly on the Internet where many new scams are appearing.

World Wide Web

For most people the Internet is the World Wide Web (WWW or Web) and email. The Web displays page on computer screens using HTML (HyperText Markup Language). It enables one page to be linked to another by hypertext links, and so allows the user to 'Surf the Web' moving effortlessly from page to page, from Web site to site, wherever they may be in the world. This Web is still growing exponentially and contains billions of pages.

Search engines & Directories

As the Internet grows it becomes more difficult to find your way around. When searching for information the usual answer is to use a search engine or directory. A search engine usually finds the information it contains by sending out crawlers (fiendish pieces of software that visit and index Web pages) and by submissions by Web site owners. The user enters a number of search words or phrases into the search engine which produces a string of possible links. The best search engine is www.google.co.uk. It is fast and relatively comprehensive.

A directory provides a different service by providing a classification structure with real people deciding which sites should be listed, if at all. Yahoo is well known but the best directory is www.dmoz.com where an army of volunteer editors peruse pages and make selections to add to the directory.

It is helpful to understand how the search engine you use really works. Does it only accept information from advertisers or is it attached to your ISP (Internet Service Provider)? If so the information it provides may be biased. Be wary (again).

There is a good 'Idiot's Guide to Search Engines' book and plenty of Web sites that offer useful advice on using search engines and directories, not least the sites that house the engines. Make sure you know and understand some of the principles. Most engines use Boolean search logic and it will help to understand how that works. You just need to know a few basic principles that rely upon being able to add, subtract and multiply.

Be Specific

Tell the search engine exactly what you are looking for. Use a short phrase or name initially that best describes your needs. If you don't know how to spell a word then the * can be used as a wildcard, substituting for the unknown character.

The + Symbol

The + symbol allows pages to be found that contain two or more words. A search for Lockwood + Ross will produce only pages that contain both words.

Remember that the initial search can be refined. Google has a special link for this at the bottom of the first search page, to search within the search.

The - Symbol

Use this to exclude certain words. Ian Rankin is known as a crime writer but has he written anything else? A search for Rankin - crime may produce results.

Quotation Marks

The + and - signs will produce (or not) words that appear on a page but they may not be near each other. A phrase within quotation marks may help, "Lockwood swimming" cuts down the search pages considerably.

Incidentally Google is run under a Linux operating system and is very fast, two statements that may be related.

The site at www.searchenginewatch.com has plenty of tips and a mountain of useful information about search engines. It will tell you how to discover how many other sites are linked to the site you are viewing, an important measure of its viability.

Site Assessment

Having found the site on a search engine or by clicking through from a link or even by typing the eddress into the top line of the browser you will be taken to its opening page.

The Internet brings a new dimension to our view of the world. Most of the information we receive has been filtered in some form; newspapers have editors; governments have spin merchants; children have teachers; television serves potatoes. The Internet is not like that - we are required to think for ourselves. Every page displayed on that computer screen in front of your eyes needs to be evaluated.

Whenever you visit a new site let your eyes scan across the opening pages while your brain assesses the validity of the site. You may have some previous knowledge about the individual, company or organisation and so assumptions can be made. For a new site it is necessary to look a little closer. There are many fakes, frauds and tricksters on the Net. Don't be scared as they are not a real problem, indeed can add amusement and variety to a dull world. They help us realise we are having to think, for ourselves, and that may be a new experience. Look carefully and the site will present a number of signals that can be used in evaluation;

> Site design - is it professional and glossy or clearly put together by an amateur.

> Domain name - is the site URL recognisable and easily traceable. A site that promises the earth that is run on a free server - with a URL that is not that of the site owner - must lose credibility. Is this site really as important as it suggests?

> Ownership - is it immediately clear who owns and runs the site. Look for name, address, personal photographs, email links, privacy statements and 'who we are' pages.

Immediate message - what is this site doing? Selling, providing information, a personal page or just a bit of fun? That immediate first reaction can be relied upon. Don't be prepared to compromise. If it looks dodgy - it probably is - so click away. There are millions of other sites to explore.

Information required - increasingly sites are requiring visitors to register in order to access the information on the site. Consider that request seriously before supplying your personal details. One trick is to use a different name when responding to doubtful sites, and to use a free email service such as that at Hotmail or Yahoo, so you can track developments and discard the free email eddress later. Some sites require an excess of information and there is no reason why you shouldn't question the site - send an email asking why they want such detail. We have become a passive people too willing to accept what we are given, the Net shows that we need to question.

As this book is written the European Union are deciding whether Web site owners can place cookies on your computer. These allow the site to collect - and possibly sell on - information you provide. Consider the following;

Are they registered under the Data Protection Acts?

Look at the site design, as it can provide useful clues about the owners and their intentions. Some sites seem set to annoy. What possible use is a page that takes ages to display on screen only to say, 'click here' to enter the site? Graphic design and technical gizmo may be hiding shallow purpose.

When was the site last updated, do the links work,

is it recognised by other sites? Some search engines will allow link searches, try putting the expression link:author.co.uk in the search engine box, obviously substituting 'author.co.uk' for the domain name of your choice to see how many other sites link to the site.

Your Internet

One day we may all be issued with a name or number that will identify us in every part of our lives. Until that time we are known in many different ways; name, address, National Insurance Number, telephone, bank account, works number. Most of these remain unchanged for a number of years. They are the marks by which we become known. I am Trevor Lockwood, I live in Suffolk, telephone number 01394 273388, email trevor@author.co.uk and so it goes on. It is a major trauma to change all these details when we move house, change jobs or bank accounts. With every move we lose touch with part of our old world.

Yet people change email eddresses without a thought and create wonderful Web sites on space provided free by an ISP. Never a thought seems to be given to long-term stability and traceability. Moving to a new email eddress or Web site can be disastrous. Contacts will be lost and the important difference between Internet contacts and most of those forged elsewhere is that, in many cases, the email or web site owner does not realise *they are listed* as a contact. Once lost they will be gone forever and these contacts may have been the most important you've ever had. Make sure you can be found.

Domain Name

The licence to use a domain name, like author.co.uk, is easy to obtain and is cheap, you only have to ask us while waving a cheque book. Buy your own domain. It can be used to create a permanent email eddress of your own. I have a number of email eddresses, including whoever@author.co.uk, that are all channelled through a BT email account. If one day I decide to move away from BT you will not notice the difference as the ISP holding the author.co.uk domain name will be asked to point all emails from that name to the new email ISP account.

A domain name can also be used as a Web site eddress.

www.author.co.uk is better than the 'free' site provided by my email ISP at www.btinternet.com/~lockwood. One looks professional and costs money to maintain, the other is largely unidentifiable yet still costs money, albeit that charge is hidden with the email charges.

Web Site

All writers should have a Web site. No arguments, all writers need a Web site. To provide an alternative to 'free' sites that make no clear statement about the site owner we provide a facility at author.co.uk that allows writers to create a Web site at an identifiable location such as www.author.co.uk/whatsisname.

Your domain name can also be pointed at those pages; www.suffolk-writers.co.uk and www.lesleycookman.co.uk are really to be found respectively at www.author.co.uk/suffolk and www.author.co.uk/lesleycookman. It's not perfect but better than obscurity or the expense and trouble of maintaining your own site.

Once established your Web site can be used as a promotional catalogue that will help sell your wares. It is a reference point where you can maintain a wide range of material. It can contain a personal biography, a regular press release, a calendar of events, details of publications with links to online bookstores, a selection of the better reviews, synopses of MSS, sample chapters, even whole books can be included on the site.

Having created the Web site make sure that everyone knows it exists. It must be added to every piece of literature you create; letterheads, business cards, leaflets, press releases. It must also be added to your email signature. Look at the Tools section of your email program to set up that important signature.

And Then ...

The domain licence has been obtained, a Web site created, and every email carries your personal signature. You are still rather like a new scarecrow in a field. All dressed up with nowhere to go - because nobody knows you exist. They must be told.

Send an email message to everyone you know, and a few that you don't, to tell them the site exists and to suggest they note your lovely new email eddress. Send individual messages, they may take longer but friends must not be herded around like a herd of sheep. Be aware that copying email eddresses to other people may also be a breach of data protection legislation, although it is possible to blind copy the message to everyone while only sending it to yourself.

Submit the Web site details to as many search engines as you can. Despite the claims of the many submission programs evidence still suggests that the best way to tell a search engine about your site is to visit each search engine in turn, and submit the information. It's boring and so we offer that service at author.co.uk as part of our contribution to the Boring Jobs Campaign.

Ask suitable sites to create links to your pages and build a page to contain links to any number of useful sites. Remember that your reputation will depend upon the quality of the sites to which links are created.

Web Design

Keep it simple. Web designers will suggest that all sorts of wonderful devices will make the site sing however research suggests that;

> New visitors wait 6 seconds for the opening page to display before they click away *for ever*.

> Individual pages should be kept below 50Kb in size

Each page should have a Title and (at least) Description and Keywords Metatabs that are hidden messages in the <head> tag that are used by search engines.

Lines of text should be no longer than 70 characters. We can't or won't read across the screen.

Pages are scanned by users. They are not really *read*. Keep navigation pages simple.

Colours chosen are important, choose with care. Cool professional blue, fiery exciting red.

Moving images are considered annoying. Use sparingly (if at all).

Users need a recognisable navigation system that is found on all pages to move around the site.

Most users are working with relatively old equipment.

Look at well-visited sites, such as Yahoo and BBC. They offer simple clear displays.

Make sure that all Web pages conform to www.w3.org standards and that the needs of disabled users have been properly considered.

Email

This is the vital chord that links us all together. Email is a marvellous tool combining immediacy like a telephone call with the permanency of a written letter. It has some weaknesses. The volume of messages received at author.co.uk every day is overwhelming and it is too easy to forget about an important message as it scrolls out of site pushed away by a mountain of Spam.

Once again the basic advice is to read the Help pages of your chosen email program. They all offer a surprising range of options. One useful default will direct emails from specified senders to a particular folder. That can separate important messages, from your family, perhaps your boss, from the inconsequential mass.

Signature

Do ensure that every email you send contains your email signature; this is a short addition at the end of your email message. At the very least it should contain your name and Web site eddress. It could also have a short quotation, a line or two of a poem or links to your very favourite agent or publisher.

SPAM

These are unsolicited emails that are sent via email; often they are trying to sell some products but they may contain well-meaning messages or be attempts to cajole the recipient to take some action. Whatever the content, they are sent unsolicited and are more than a nuisance, they pose a real threat to the efficacy of the system.

We all receive direct mail (often called junk mail) by conventional postal services every day. Most of us have an ambivalent attitude towards some of the material but it does help to support our postal service (now in great danger in the UK) it also elicits a response (2% sales response is often considered worthwhile) and we can always request that it is not sent to our address.

Electronic junk mail (SPAM) is proving more difficult to control. Part of the problem is the ease with which Spam can be sent, not just to one eddress but to many millions at a time. There are a number of basic steps that will reduce, if not prevent, this deluge of material.

Don't Buy the products advertised

Also do not try to sell anything by mass unsolicited bulk e-mail. Only the companies selling bulk email programs ever make any money.

Prevention is better than cure

It is very difficult to have your eddress removed from a list. At the end of many spam messages there is an unsubsribe option urging you to send an email to be removed from the list. Do NOT respond to this message, as it confirms that you have a valid and operating email eddress and as a result even more spam messages will arrive.

Web Sites

An email eddress displayed on a Web site invites spam, as there are many programs designed to trawl emails from sites. Instead of a direct email link place a Form on the page that site visitors can complete and send to you (don't forget to ask for their email address).

Chain Letters

These can take many forms, some are illegal pyramid schemes that suggest you can become rich by selling partnerships in the scheme to your friends, who in turn sell to their friends.

One increasingly common form of round robin letter warns of a computer virus. Sent to one person it urges them to contact all their friends to warn them of the dire consequences of this latest, even more virulent, virus. Invariably these are hoaxes, and are causing more damage to the Net than the 57,000 known viruses as they hog enormous amounts of bandwidth and so slow down the entire system. Make sure you have a good anti-virus program installed, and that it is updated regularly.

The National Consumers League's National Fraud

Information Center www.fraud.org is a useful site providing information about Internet and telemarketing fraud.

Superb Offers

The Internet is a not a latter-day gold mine. It is not a way to make easy money, although many of the spam messages suggest that a super new life awaits if you'll only subscribe to the scam they present. Be warned that any message that says it is legal or that it can make you (a complete stranger) fabulously wealthy is lying. Why should you be chosen to receive such largesse? Ignore these people.

Mailing Lists and Newsgroups

Email eddresses can be harvested from mailing lists. This is a difficult area as other members of the list may wish to use your email to contact you off-list. It is possible to conceal your email eddress by sending a 'SET CONCEAL' command to the list address. Contact the mailing list administrator, who should be able to set up this facility.

It's not considered good form to post anonymously to a Newsgroup but once again junk emailers obtain their targets from these groups. Your mailing program may allow you to set up an anonymous 'reply-to' eddress. That's possible with Netscape but the majority of the Net world is now using another browser.

That basic rule of *never* responding to spam messages is very important with newsgroups as your reply may be sent to dozens of other newsgroups who have also received the original spam. Forward the spam message to manews.admin.net-abuse.misc who will ensure it is cancelled from all newsgroups.

It is possible to surf the Web anonymously. Programs, such as those at www.anonymizer.com and http://nethush.com/ allow you to surf the Web anonymously, without leaving a trail of personal information across the

Web. It is possible to build up a profile about your life-style by monitoring your activity on the Web. Don't be too disturbed but do remember that as you surf the Web your movements can be tracked, and recorded. Very often a Web site will place a cookie on your computer's hard drive. While these are often innocuous make sure your browser is formatted to warn whenever a cookie is about to be placed as there may be some sites you visit that should not be allowed to know too much.

The Freesite http://www.thefreesite.com/ includes a good list of 'anonymous freebies'; programs that can help you ensure privacy online

How to Complain

You can forward the junk email, with complete headers, to the Internet Service Provider (ISP) of the sender (unless the sender has an AOL address, and many people do still use this closed community approach then send to tosemail1@aol.com)

An easier, if not better, way may be to register with Abuse.Net www.abuse.net and also join the Campaign Against Unsolicited Commercial Email, www.euro.cauce.org who ask you to forward your Spam to them at spamrecycle@ChooseYourMail.com.

Personally I use Spamcop.net www.spamcop.net and pay a small sum for membership that allows me to submit the rubbish I receive where it is checked online, and I can then choose which ISP should be warned that they are involved in this vile trade.

For Newsgroups there is an unmoderated list at news.admin.net-abuse.e-mail (NANAE) that discusses of possible abuses of email and news.admin.net-abuse.announce is a newsgroup for the discussion of events associated with net abuse.

The European Union, bless their cotton socks, are trying

to pass legislation to ban unsolicited emails. Let's hope that large corporate interests don't swamp the politicians.

Firewalls

Increasingly hackers are trying to gain access to your computer often so they can use your email and computer's identity to send spam messages. Those with ISDN or ADSL (broadband) access are most at risk but firewall software is effective and cheap. You can check the vulnerability of your computer at

HackYourself.com, http://hackyourself.com/ also has good basic advice. Other useful sites include the Elephants Toolbox, www.cotse.com and Shields Up, https://grc.com/ that will check the security of your computer and show its vulnerability to hackers. The https: shows that this is a secure site, and this format is often seen on pages demanding online payment.

Contact Lists

Many sites exist to provide information about people. It's a useful service, widely used by those wishing to trace long-lost friends and relatives or debtors. However these sites are also widely used by spammers. You can check such sites and ask to have your name removed, most will comply although the Net has no controlling legislation that makes them take action. Most of the major search engines include such a service.

Copyright

Copyright need not be owned by the author or their descendants. Copyright is a saleable commodity, and publishers often retain some rights.

Infringing copyright can incur serious penalties. If you take photocopies from printed material, record television programmes off-air, run discotheques or play records or tapes in a public place, then copyright must be considered. Writers using the Internet risk losing control of their work and must take whatever steps they can to prevent unauthorised use.

Copyright exists in all literary, dramatic, musical or artistic work in whatever format it is produced, including audio or videotape. In England and Wales the law on the subject is mainly contained within the Copyright, Designs and Patents Act 1988.

Broadly speaking there is no copyright in a title, in a pseudonym or in the bare bones of a plot or an idea. There are few formalities in UK or any other country that complies with the Berne Copyright Union. The © symbol together with the year of production and the owner's name are sufficient. Recently the US has decided that the © can be replaced with the word, Copyright, but that may not be accepted universally.

Prove it Exists

Even though copyright is automatically acquired it is wise to establish some evidence that the work was in existence at a certain time. Some people post a copy to themselves, in a sealed envelope that is NEVER opened. Or deposit a copy at the bank or with a solicitor, upon a dated receipt. There is a deposit service operated in London.

The copyright symbol © is the notice of the Universal Copyright Convention, of which Great Britain and Northern Ireland and over sixty other countries are members. Work carrying this notice is protected in every member state.

In the UK copyright remains yours as writer and publisher, and for most works for 70 years from the end of the year of the author's death. There are some variations to this; and The Society of Authors produces a useful Quick Guide for their members.

Since 1989 copyright in the USA has become clearer and now follows the accepted conventions. Prior to that time there was a morass of regulations. Look at the US government site http://www.loc.gov/copyright/ where there is plenty of useful information.

Myths

Copyright protection is a minefield with nuances that extend far beyond the scope of this book. There are several myths that should be dismissed. Displaying information produced by others without permission even though no charge is made is still breach of copyright. Copy found on Usenet, in emails or on Web sites is not in the public domain, it is still the property of the owner. It is possible to use a small extract but ownership should be acknowledged. If you do not know the owner then the material should not be used. Basing your story on characters in copyrighted work, so-called derivative works, is illegal unless you intend to parody or poke fun.

Beware of sending your work to the growing plethora of sites that offer to display your work for sale. This is not to dismiss the concept but do read the contract conditions very carefully as copyright control may be granted to the site, sometimes for ever. Take time to consider the full implications. Joan Collins signed away her rights to Dynasty in an ill-considered moment and lost a fortune. Do not do the same.

There are a number of useful associations and sites that will provide advice and information. The Authors Licensing & Copyright Society, see www.alcs.co.uk is the UK rights management society that collects and distributes fees for writers whose works have been photocopied, broadcast or recorded. It does have some good advice on electronic rights. These contracts require care, they will often be treated as subsidiary rights to a printed document contract but this can leave the writer exposed, who should be wary and certainly not sign away exclusive rights.

Electronic Works

Works that will be used in digital formats are probably best dealt with by granting licences for a specific use rather than through sale. Words may be interpreted differently and care must be taken. First publication rights should not, always, mean print; and electronic rights and even 'non-exclusive rights' granted to a Web site owner may result in the transfer of rights and interest.

This is a fast-moving world and beyond the scope of this book, but be aware that your copy can be presented in any number of different ways. It is not enough to understand that electronic rights means production of an ebook version of the printed book, as it may mean so much more. Take advice and be wary (we keep saying!).

Electronic rights are often divided into off-line uses; CD-ROM, multi-media, video, DVD, film and on-line; Web display, CD-I, laser using digital, optical, magnetic storage retrieval and distribution systems all of which may allow the material to be copied, displayed and retrieved, modified, edited, adapted, combined with other material and even printed; as single or multiple copies. And that is just a small selection of the systems known today. The morrow will undoubtedly bring new developments.

Web sites

It makes sense to add the copyright symbol, year of production and author/owner name to all documents you produce. That also includes Web sites but do make sure you really do own the copyright to all the material displayed on Web pages. A page consists of several elements; text, graphics, scripts, data and code. If you created everything then ownership can be assumed. It becomes complicated when each element that is used to make up the page is considered separately. It may be necessary to contact the provider of clip art or of a scanned photograph or image or if a Web design company is involved.

Passing over Copyright

This is an area where writers must take some care. Too many have signed away rights in the euphoria of acceptance. Rights go something like this;

> Right of paternity: right of author to be identified whenever a work is published, performed or broadcast.
> Right of integrity: right of an author to object to derogatory treatment of their work.
> Right not to have the work falsely attributed to you.

These moral rights cannot be assigned to someone else, but they can be waived by the author in writing. Take advice before doing so.

First British Serial Rights

Indicates that this work has never been published before in any form. As authors we hold on to these and they are normally granted solely for that purpose. That is, the licence to publish once for the first time in the United Kingdom.

Second serial rights

May be sold to trade papers, house journals or local papers, for which the author should expect no less than 75% of the fees so obtained.

Third rights

Are for the publishers of anthologies with author expecting 60%.

Subsidiary Rights

The range is legion, including;

Paperback rights with the book licensed to another publisher. This is so common that a percentage is usually included in the original hardback contract - make sure it is there.

Book club rights: A percentage payable is often agreed between publisher and author. It should be no less than 50% of any royalty paid by the book club, and if the publisher is involved in producing the books should be no less than 10% of the gross sale price.

Trade paperback mail order rights. Where a percentage is normally agreed dependent upon the original deal.

Digest: Book condensation, low-cost reprint rights, American Book Club in publisher's territory. Normally no less than 50%

Educational editions and hardback reprint rights. To be agreed dependent upon the deal

Large print rights: usually 60%

Same language territorial rights and film, broadcasting, to serialise and translate, to adapt, abridge, anthologise, digest, mechanical and reprographic reproduction, electronic publishing, charitable, merchandising, authorising Braille recordings or as a talking book or micro-filming for handicapped people to use for non-commercial purposes - and more, all subject to separate negotiation.

How to dispose of these rights is a subject slowly being addressed by the authorities. That process is slow, dependent upon an interchange of information - but is one step forward that does not exist today for the small publisher in the UK.

Contracts

For the author dealing with a trade publisher the contract conditions imposed may be onerous, and should be closely examined before agreement is reached.

The publisher will probably try to demand exclusive right to sub-licence rights within an exclusive territory (which may be worldwide). They may add provisos, they may request the author's approval, but then insist that it cannot be unreasonably withheld (whatever that may mean). Copies of any agreements for the sale of rights should be made available, and the original contract should make some mention of the recompense due to the author in the event of the sale of rights.

What is meant by digital or electronic must still be clearly defined, and that is not easy as technology keeps coming up with new ideas all the time.

All these rights may be passed over to another for a consideration. It is that consideration that forms the contract, without which there is no deal in English law. It can take many forms, but usually means money passes from one hand to another. Make sure it does. Note also that a contract need not last for ever. The copyright licence can be passed over for a period of time, then revert back to the author. Make sure that a time limit is included.

Permissions

The Internet is showing us all that information is easy to obtain. Just go to a site, cut and paste the information and turn it into your own. It's getting easier to become a writer.

It doesn't really work that way and acting in such a cavalier fashion will quickly lose your reputation, and remember we all live in a very small world and you may get away with for a time but eventually justice will prevail.

When are permissions likely to be needed?

When some material is to be used in a collection or anthology, however short and where a 'quotation' is to be used for purposes that the Copyright Act describes as for 'the purposes of criticism or review'. Life gets even more complicated because the Copyright Act (and this is a Westminster Act of Parliament, broadly speaking applying to England & Wales but it has similarities elsewhere) talks of 'fair dealing' without defining what that means. If a quote is to be used for criticism or review you need not ask the permission of the owner of the copyright but give some acknowledgement.

What is 'fair'? Likely to be interpreted fairly liberally (but don't rely upon me for anything) but the length of the quote, its relevance to your own work and the amount quoted in comparison to your own work are clearly important. You can't start with a phrase like; and Joe Bloggs says, '....' then go on to quote the entire chapter (or book)!

The Publishers Association and the Society of Authors in Great Britain are content with quotes under 400 words, or a series of extracts, none of which exceeds 300 words, up to a total of 800 words of prose, or 40 lines of poetry, provided this is not more than a quarter of the whole poem. Seems reasonable and remember the quotes are only there for the purposes of 'criticism and review'.

Appendix A of Publishing Agreements: A book of Precedents (4th Edition) gives details of the agreement reached by Publishers Association and The Society of Authors in 1957;

From a copyright prose work

1. for any extract longer than 400 words
2. for a series of extracts totalling more than 800 words
3. for a series of extracts of which any one extract is more than 300 words
4. for a series of extracts comprising together one-quarter or more of a complete poem.

From a copyright work of poetry

1. for an extract of more than 40 lines
2. for a series of extracts totalling more than 40 lines
3. for an extract comprising one-quarter or more of a complete poem
4. for a series of extracts comprising together one-quarter or more of a complete poem

Anything more 'substantial' (the Act again being imprecise) and you should ask permission. Certainly do not rely upon anything in this book if you are faced with a serious decision, seek suitable advice.

Getting Permission

Write to the copyright holder - perhaps construct a form to send to the publisher in the first instance, a 'Permission Form' asking that it be forwarded to the relevant authority, provide a copy of what you want to include, say what the work will be, ask for confirmation that the work is still in copyright (do not assume - do not let them assume - ask).

If you are starting to write a work using copyright material, think about permissions now! Leaving it to the last minute may result in a reply that says, 'No' or (more likely) 'Yes, but we want £10,000'.

Editing your book

With sincere apologies to the worthies upon whom writers rely, the word 'editing' is expanded to include several separate functions.

Proofreading

A proofreader will read the manuscript and highlight errors (usually in red) in spelling, punctuation and grammar.

Copy Editing

This is a step forward as the copy editor will redline and also make changes to the manuscript.

Editing

In overall control the editor will make suggestions or even dictate necessary manuscript changes to the author, in order to make clear to the reader the intended meaning.

Who Will Edit?

The obvious answer is that the writer cannot edit his or her own work before it finally goes to print. You will pass over the same mistakes time and again, and get too absorbed in the content to pay real attention to the editing process.

This cannot be an instant course in editing but writers should have some understanding of the work of an editor.

The Editing Process

Editors do more than checking grammar. An editor will polish the writing style, often increasing the pace and so help to capture the reader's interest. They will also keep a careful eye on consistency and help to avoid the pitfalls of libel and copyright infringement.

An editor will be aware of the whole book and can give invaluable advice. They may say a title should be kept short, perhaps no more than five words, and these should reflect the content of the book. They may suggest you use strong verbs in the title and for chapter headings.

A foreword by some luminary may look good on the cover, but these sage words are rarely read. In many non-fiction books even the first chapter is left unread as the eager reader dives into the body of the book for real information. Nevertheless, imitate the best books you know because first impressions count.

Pages of text can be very boring so break up the text with: tables, charts, illustrations, checklists and use bullets. To further break up the text insert a sub-heading at frequent intervals.

Your Fiction

If you're writing fiction you should be well practised in creating a good read. It is a craft and much of this book is suggesting it is an art form. Too many writers dive in, producing a scrappy manuscript without bothering to understand basic facts. Learn the rules before successfully breaking them. If you self-publish before you've learned what you need to know, that lesson will be hard on your pocket.

A new novelist should try to introduce the main character in the first page, preferably in the first paragraph or at least grab the reader's attention with the first few words.

It should follow throughout the book as the writer maintains tension, so building a page-turner that cannot be put down. Descriptive prose is necessary but must be used with due restraint. See the chapter 'Visualise' for more on this arena.

Tenses and viewpoints should be consistent throughout - or the change must be made patently obvious. This is discussed in 'Style'.

Characters should have believable motives, actions and relationships - as discussed in 'Talk and Tell' - and the events that move the plot along must be credible. Each character must be well-described, or better still, shown to be well-rounded. Relationships, especially love, must be clearly demonstrated not just stated. Balancing every element of a situation with just the right amount of detail and pace takes practice. All good writing is explicit where it matters.

Read dialogue out loud to make sure it sounds real.

Plots need the minimum number of characters to make the story flow, so condense the actions of minor players into one character whenever possible. You don't walk into a room crowded with strangers and get to know them all at once, so don't expect your readers to do the equivalent. Each conflict should be introduced properly and milked to bring out everything it has to offer. There may be subtleties that link up with precedents and antecedents, making a tight construction and a startling analogy with life. Too many extraneous incidents weaken interest in the main story.

Ensure the reader knows the timeline of the story. Where are they now, and how does that relate to other events in the tale? A brief sentence will normally be enough to make everything clear, but it's surprisingly easy to forget what your reader doesn't know.

However enchanted you may be by the style of a famous author, don't try to make an exact copy. Develop your own voice.

Check spelling, sentence structure and grammar, because the manuscript must be the very best you can muster before it leaves your hands. Also ensure you know the meaning of words employed.

Know your intended audience. These are basic points that every professional fiction editor will tell you, and if you haven't taken them all on board before going for publication, your first attempt will teach you. This chapter may be about editing but professional editors will gain little from these paragraphs as they are intended to provide inspiration to those rank amateurs; writers.

The editor will be concerned with proofreading and style,

will be correcting errors in time, quotations and making sure the fashions of the period are properly portrayed. If you go for self-publishing, you should ensure these jobs are properly completed. An editor will also be concerned with the continuity and flow of the book. This volume has two authors, and hopefully you will recognise two distinct writing styles. There is an intentional Ying and a Yang.

A novel will require a different editing influence than for a non-fiction book; for the reader must believe in the plot, the atmosphere of the book, the characters and the dialogue.

Using an Editor

At author.co.uk we have a short list of editors and proofreaders who we know personally, and have used (or misused) for a project at some time. The best source of professional workers is at the Society of Editors and Proofreaders www.sfep.org.uk.

Employ an editor who knows and understands your subject and make sure you both understand the tasks that have to be completed, and when, and at what cost.

Make a checklist of your requirements;

What do you need to be supplied?

How much will you pay?

What expenses are claimable, and how will they be claimed?

When should invoices be submitted, under what circumstances?

When will payment be made - within 30 days?

What is the deadline - what penalties for late supply?

Format of delivery; disk, CD-ROM, PageMaker file?

Consider rights licensing, insurance and more.

Expect to pay editors good money for they provide an essential and skilled service. And do listen to the advice they give.

Indexing

The work is now complete except that somewhere in the production plan you will have made provision for the work to be indexed. If you try to create an index using a word-processing program you quickly realise that it is not as easy as it looks, and for a substantial work a professional indexer should be employed.

An index is a detailed guide to the information and ideas in a document. There is a British Standard that defines an index as; 'A systematic arrangement of entries designed to enable users to locate information in a document'.

Finding Information

An index enables enquirers to find information they need or to recall half-remembered passages. It does so by providing search terms in an appropriately organised list. The terms may be single words, phrases, abbreviations, acronyms, dates, names, or any other indexable elements or concepts. The index leads to specific locations in the document, using the numbers (or other indicators) of pages, columns, sections, frames, figures, tables, paragraphs, lines or other components.

Do It Yourself?

Authors sometimes compile their own indexes but do so effectively only if they combine their subject knowledge with the skills of an index compiler, who requires the ability to analyse the text on behalf of a wide range of users who may want to locate information on a particular topic. You must have a good knowledge of the subject matter and the the ability to devise suitable terms expressing the concepts in the text concisely and precisely. Perhaps the most difficult tasks for the creative mind is the ability to organise the entries in the index in the most appropriate and retrievable fashion and the need to have a passion for accuracy.

If in doubt, use a professional indexer, preferably a member of the Society of Indexers.

Submitting to a Publisher

Professional Approach

That's what is needed; a mature and professional approach. Gardners Books, the book wholesalers who run the author.co.uk bookstore, have over 27,000 publishers on their stock list. The major sources of information about publishers are the Writers Handbook, edited by Barry Turner, and the Writers & Artists Yearbook. These annual directories contain contact details for a selection of publishers, mainly larger companies but with a sprinkling of the esoteric.

At author.co.uk we maintain a list of publishers; those who have contacted us or have agreed to accept submissions for writers. A surprising number of publishers baulk at the idea of email submissions, fearing a deluge. We believe it is easier to click an email into oblivion than dispose of the mouldering slush-pile of submitted MSS found in many publishers' offices.

The Right Publisher

The first task is to search for the right publisher. Look at your masterpiece very carefully, and then forage around in libraries, bookshops and the Internet to find similar works. Look for your competition. It's a good idea to buy some of those books and read them very carefully to discover what they have that yours may be missing, but that's another story. Having found books that match your own in approach, style and genre make a list of their publishers. This is a good place to start. Books (accountants please note) are all unique objects. We try to classify books but only rarely does one book compete directly with another. Books are individuals, they are entities in themselves and so a publisher who has accepted one romantic novel based in Liverpool may well consider another. At least someone in the company may have some sympathy for you.

Before Submission

You wouldn't go to see a prospective employer wearing dirty clothes looking slovenly and unkempt. To do so would reduce your chances of getting the job. So it is with submissions to publishers. Too often a prospective book can be rejected because it does not look good to the eye. A dog-eared MS that has clearly had a previous life in another office does not make a good impression. Use a new copy for each submission. And do use a spell-checker, then print out the submission and read it through very carefully looking for errors. Ask somebody else to check for mistakes. Print in a readable serif font, perhaps Times New Roman or Garamond, double-spaced lines, with plenty of margin space at one side of the page to allow for scribbled notes. Ensure there is a Header (or footer) note with your name, contact email or telephone, the title of the work and that it says 'this is Page X of XX pages'. Make life easy for the reader.

What to Send

In the first instance 'not a lot'. Having selected a number of likely prospects write each of them a personal letter. It may help to phone the publisher first; to establish whether they are accepting submissions and find the name of the person who will handle the job initially. Publishers' telephonists are invaluable sources of information, so take them into your confidence. Use that gently submissive tone when asking them a question, treat them as friends and crack a joke or two at your own expense. In short do anything you can to ensure they are on your side and will become willing to put you in touch with the real movers in the company.

You need to know which publishers are likely to be interested in your work, and who within that company will deal with your submission.

Many publishers' Web sites now contain guidelines for authors; find them, read them and try to conform to the stated requirements. Put yourself in the publisher's seat. Would you really put good money into this book? And it may be more than just money they are risking; the company reputation, even the commissioning editor's own job may be at stake, if they make a serious mistake.

Be convinced that all the publishers on your list will be begging to take your manuscript. Send each one the personally addressed letter together with a synopsis and a sample chapter or two.

The Package to Send

The letter is short and sweet. It says who you are, how you can be contacted, that you have titles, maybe articles, in print (if relevant) and that your latest book will sell because ..... Consider carefully what will make your book sell. Condense that essence into one short sentence.

The synopsis is also short and sweet. It describes the book; where it is going, how it does that, and what is the intended result. It will contain the major stepping stones through the book; perhaps using a plot description mingled with a picture of the main characters. It says how many words the MS contains, or will contain. It is the very nectar distilled from all the many hours you have laboured upon this creation. It is no more than two pages long.

The sample chapters sent will vary. Some publishers will insist upon the first two or three chapters, and so you should comply - albeit making a quiet protest if necessary, and enclosing an additional chapter that will emphasise your point. The samples will be representative of the whole work; to show how well your words flow along the pages, how easy the work is to read, how gripping the tale.

These three elements, neatly packaged together, with a Treasury tag or simple heat binding to hold together the synopsis or sample chapters, can then be sent off to the selected publishers. I don't subscribe to the idea that you must only send your work to one publisher at a time. That is a myth generated by those who do not want authors to get involved in an auction. But authors must relish the chance of two or more publishers saying they wish to publish the book. More than one means that negotiation can take place.

It may be wise to send it to a small selection initially, and to await their response (if it comes quickly enough). The replies may give you some indication of how to improve subsequent submissions.

Keep a careful record of where, when and to whom submissions were sent and of the replies. While waiting for a reply start work on the next manuscript. That last MS was not your best work, that is still to come.

Literary Agents

What do they do?

Literary agents provide writers with contacts and a measure of experience and some knowledge of contracts. For 10% (or more) they act as an intermediary between author and publisher. For that money they should know which publishers best suit your work and provide legal and intellectual property advice. The Society of Authors will also provide very useful advice (if you are a published author) and there is the camaraderie and information that comes from membership of an august association.

Good writing comes first and successful writers have agents, for agents live upon success. There are very few agents who want to assist struggling author-publishers. They may be assured of a great welcome when they do.

How to find one

Agents are considered to be very necessary by those relying upon the commercial publishing trade, especially in America. They do a very good job for many writers. The Association of Authors' Agents, 62 Grafton Way, London W1P 5LD maintain a code of professional practice, and may help with lists of their members.

Agents are liked by editors for they place an effective barrier between publisher and author. It's rather like the client, butcher, slaughterhouse relationship. The mooing and baaing of authors in torment is kept at a step removed.

Bad Agents

As with vanity or subsidy publishers there are unscrupulous persons who describe themselves as agents so they can make a profit not by selling books to publishers, but by selling 'services' to writers. This an unethical approach;

beware of agencies demanding excessive reading or representation fees. This is a difficult area in which to provide definitive advice. The Literary Consultancy, for example, provides a literary criticism service and may also act as an author's agent. They charge fees for their excellent services that can also include agency support although that is not their primary service. The answer is to exercise caution before making a commitment. Always seek advice from others, and make sure you talk to other authors using the agency's services.

Be suspicious of a publisher who recommends an agency. It may be that the publisher uses an agent as a clearance or initial screening device but be very wary if that agency subsequently asks for money for 'editorial' services.

How to find an Agent

So far most literary agencies have avoided the Internet, fearing an avalanche of unsolicited manuscripts. That's an anomalous stance as an agent relies upon new work from authors. For now there is natural fear of the unknown and perhaps they will slowly realise that it is easier to delete an email than to have to store, handle, return or dispose of a slush pile of manuscripts.

Don't be afraid to telephone to ask if they are taking on new writers. Try to talk to the agent who deals with your sort of writing. Members of the Association of Authors' Agents are the best place to start.

Treat an approach to an agent in the same way as you would submit to a publisher. Prepare a synopsis: a sharp succinct description of your work. Have an introductory letter, preferably addressed to a named person within the agency. Let it be brief. Include one, two or three of the best chapters in your proposed book - no more. Usual rules apply; typed or word-processed text, double spaced, one side of the paper, each sheet to contain your working title, your name, and page numbers.

Provided an agent is found then be prepared to face their criticism or comments about your work.

The market for that first book is difficult; the market is fickle as the publishing industry continues to agglomerate and the UK bookselling industry destroys itself in search of short-term gain.

This is a business

Recognise that in wanting to use the services of an agent you are prepared to enter a commercial world. Your concern will be to produce a product that sells. A good example of a new author recognising this real world is Julian Stockwin. An ex-seaman he loved writing about naval history, and his supportive wife suggested he should make a serious attempt at becoming an author. A large amiable bearded man he is looks as if he was born to stand beforethe mast. He wrote his first book, Kydd, and was halfway through the second before approaching the Blake Friedmann agency. He was able to present not just the manuscript for one book, but had nearly finished the second with plans outlined for books three and four. Carole Blake saw a gap emerging in the market and negotiated a substantial four-book deal for Julian.

Julian Stockwin's preparation was professional and organised. He writes for an established genre whose market is known. He was fortunate that the established leader of that specific interest group had just died, leaving a gap in the market. Julian knew his subject and writes a good page-turner. Success looks assured.

The literary agent provides an interface between the writer and publisher, bringing knowledge, experience and contacts to the scribbler while acting as a barrier against a deluge of unsuitable material and as a source of reliable information for the publisher. They walk a careful line, particularly when handling a new or unknown writer. Once success is assured they act as a seasoned personal assistant and negotiator for the recognised writer.

Ebooks

Electronic books are becoming an important element within the digital revolution. As with all new processes there have been a number of wild promises and some significant changes over the last year. It is still moving very fast.

In the beginning an ebook was little more than a word-processed file made available as a downloadable file on the Internet. Now we see a variety of programs that allow material to be displayed; and increasingly these are becoming multi-media events. This is not a world that is constrained like a printed book. No clear standards have yet emerged but there are significant developments. An Open Ebook Standard has been internationally agreed but is under continuous development as new products and problems need to be addressed.

It was necessary to move beyond providing a downloadable word-processed document so as to provide a measure of protection for the writer and/or copyright owner, and to ensure security of the product. Copyright is assisted with programs such as Adobe Acrobat that also allows universal availability. Any computer that has Adobe Acrobat Reader loaded (and it is free) can read an Acrobat.pdf file. The document will display in exactly the way its creator intended on any computer. This is so effective that Acrobat files are now used as originating artwork by printers, as they do not allow errors.

The universality of Acrobat documents brings, in itself, a problem for ebook sellers. They may sell one copy but can exercise little control of what happens to that file once it has been sold. Unlike books computer files can be copied and transferred via the Internet so one copy can quickly become many thousands.

Ebook Reader software

This weakness (in commercial terms) led to another approach, currently led by Adobe and Microsoft, both of whom now have Ebook Reader software. These programs use a simplified form of HTML (the language of the Web) and an encryption program. They allow easy display of ebooks on a wide range of computers and offer one important element that's missing from the Acrobat.pdf file; in that they can be restricted to use on just one, or two, machines. Details of the purchaser of such an ebook are recorded at the time of purchase and the ebooks are loaded to one machine.

The ebooks produced by these programs can be displayed on any computer, provided that it contains the correct software. New fonts have been developed to allow easy on-screen reading and the ebook navigation systems are simple to understand and use. They do offer flexibility and this is becoming increasingly important. Creating a document to be read by an Ebook Reader requires that it be formatted to be read on a standard computer, a hand-held, on Web TV and elsewhere. New generations of ebooks will lead us into a multi-media environment. The first version of the MS Reader contained a text reader, that would read the text for you once you decided it was too tiring to read the words on the screen.

There is an understandable desire by the originators of ebooks to retain control. Clearly there is no business sense in producing work that can be freely distributed, or even resold by unscrupulous vendors who have no connection with the ebook's creators.

Ebook Readers

Sitting at a desk reading from an ebook on a computer screen is not very comfortable. Forced to work with the infernal machines all day people were unlikely to do the same when they arrived home in the evening. This led to the development of hand-held readers; the Rocket ebook was an early pioneer providing a device that weighed little more than a good-sized book yet could display up to 20,000 pages of text (and simple graphics) on a small screen. It looked like a book, worked much like a book but had some important additional attributes. It could contain up to 200 books; notes could be added; and a dictionary was included, and it was backlit enabling it to be read in bed, with the covers over your head and without disturbing your partner.

These hand-held ebook readers are still progressing and at the time of writing the Hiebook has just been released, which promises to be capable of reading in a variety of formats, has an MP3 player and will add colour at some time in the future. Such machines are still relatively expensive and this is prompting other producers to look at ways of reducing costs. One device that is little more than two plastic A4 sheets separated by a chargeable layer that is just one molecule thick has been suggested. Electrify a molecule to make it turn black, switch it off to be transparent - all very simple, so they say.

These face competition from PDA's (hand-held organisers) and even game-playing machines, both of which can be adapted to display ebooks.

The basic formats in common use now are Microsoft Word, HTML: Hypertext Mark-Up Language, the coding used to create a normal Web page, the Adobe Acrobat, Glassbook/Adobe Ebook Reader, MS Reader, Rocket ebook/REB, Franklin eBookman, Palm and Handspring, Cytale and Hiebook.

Ebook Publishing

Publishing an ebook is an attractive proposition. It allows the unpublished (and unpublishable) author to produce a readable product, and established authors can resurrect old material that has been remaindered by the original publisher; and it's cheap.

It does not replace any of the existing systems. It is no substitute for the small publisher producing esoteric books. It offers a different perspective much as the radio does when compared to books, or the TV to film. Whenever new technology is introduced there has been an accommodation, a shifting of position, that eventually settles down to allow each medium to do what it does best.

For the writer the ebook offers advantages. It is not difficult to produce an ebook. Compared to a printed book production costs are very low. Marketing and distribution remain the perennial problems for the small author-publisher but there are a growing number of ebook publishers' sites, most of whom will be able to assist although not enough are yet carrying a full range of titles.

The selection process adopted by these ebook publishers varies considerably. Some will accept anything; unedited, unremarked, unworthy. Such sites often require the writer to subsidise the cost of production and authors should be wary before joining such outfits. Your superb piece of crafted work will stand alongside a load of ill-considered rubbish and may well be tainted by such contact.

Most ebook sites will display ebooks for their authors taking a commission when the book is downloaded; that is *sold* to a customer. Some sites demand a fee before the ebook is offered for sale. This is to cover the cost of producing the ebook from a word-processed text. Too many sites expect the author to have edited and proof-read the document before it is submitted. Too few sites take much interest in the content quality but that should change as the readers of ebooks make demands.

More than Fiction

There is still too much concentration, in epublishing, upon works of fiction whereas the ebook seems to offer the most attractive prospects for non-fiction works, particularly those whose information is subject to change. Lists of addresses, reference works, instruction manuals can all benefit from ebook production. A work of fiction less so, except that the ebook is cheap, can be read once and then be easily discarded.

Very few Web sites function like normal print publishers; accepting MSS, deciding to publish, then editing, proofing, producing, marketing, promoting and distributing the finished work. Instead many sites do not commission work or invite submissions from writers, they merely accept what they are sent. They exercise no editorial control and there's no filter imposed upon the slush pile of submissions. Nor do they even proof-read the work, but are content for it to be presented in its raw state. While there is a strong argument that the reader should decide and that trade publishers sometimes impose economic criteria at the expense of literary content, too many of the present ebook sites have thrown all caution to the wind and that could spell danger.

Checklist

The author wanting to use an ebook site needs to consider several factors:-

- How much money is being charged in the first instance, if any?

- What genres does the ebook site serve, and are they appropriate?

- What display formats will be available?

- Is there an understandable comprehendable submissions page?

- What is the editorial policy: how do they select and edit manuscripts?

- What percentage commission is payable to the author?

- How successful is the site at marketing the ebooks? Can they give you actual sales figures?

- Is the contract restrictive or can the author display elsewhere?

- Does the ecommerce system used by the site work efficiently?

- Will the work receive an ISBN and be promoted in any way?

- Is the site credible? How many visitors does it receive?

- Who runs the site, and are they linked to any known associations?

- Can you contact the authors already at the site? If so, send them an email that asks questions.

- When will you be paid, and how?

- Test the system, buy an ebook from your chosen site.

Be critical. Ask questions and do not rely solely upon the answers received. Talk to other authors using the site. Make sure you retain full copyright. Some sites assume all electronic rights will be granted as a result of the contract, and that can be very restrictive.

Rogues and Vagabonds

The ebook equivalent of a vanity publisher is an ever-present danger. There are plenty of sharks in the ether ready to take money from hapless writers. Every contract presented to you by an ebook publisher will be different. Read them very carefully before committing to an irretrievable disaster. The very best sites will have a large number of visitors and buyers while imposing rigorous editorial control and not ask for payment to publish. They are few and far between but do exist and are to be wholeheartedly supported.

Ebook publishing is attractive and even more so now it is being linked to print on demand publishing. The ebook is ready to be printed, and one copy at a time can now be printed. Bookshops in the future may well be an attractive mix of coffee shop, book display centre and print shop. Authors will be able to effectively reach readers. Quality will remain very important.

Selling Ebooks

However the ebook is produced it must then be sold. As with any product it is marketing, distributing and selling that can prove the most troublesome. The low cost of production does mean that the ebook publisher can take more risks than a print publisher. There is no problem of storage or distribution and they do not waste trees.

Potentially the rewards for authors can be attractive. Royalty payments vary but are usually much higher than those paid by print publishers with 30-70% often available.

Authors must get much more involved in promoting and selling their ebooks. Most ebook sites lack the personnel and experience to do much more than display your work on their own site, which is often poorly visited. There are very few ebook sites demanding exclusive contracts that can be recommended. At present no site has sufficient global coverage to guarantee any real advantage for exclusivity.

The General Picture

The Internet offers a global market; at least of those world citizens with enough money to be linked to the system. CD's do offer another method of distributing material, particularly to those who do not have an Internet connection.

There has not been an explosion of interest in ebooks, and many of the earlier sites have disappeared. That said the larger online bookstores have now started to stock ebooks, and signs are encouraging. As with all products it is the product that will attract customers and the material must be professionally produced and of the highest quality.

Many conventional print publishers appear reluctant to enter this market, indeed most are scared of the Internet altogether. They can see how print on demand will be useful and a number of the larger agglomerates are already involved with content streaming; providing snippets of content to a variety of places, creating a minefield for authors' ownership of words.

Electronically published authors now have agents, attend promotions, can be guests on the radio, television and chat rooms, and may be interviewed for articles and speak to writers' groups. Many authors are published both traditionally and electronically. Ebook authors need not just be authors who can't get published.

There are a number of websites that provide resources for writers who have already published electronically or are thinking about it.

Try one of our initiatives, the Epublishing Association www.epublish.org.uk, as we are making a small start in the UK. The site lists a number of the small British ebook publishers and we plan to work together to share information and agree common standards. Perhapsto create a Code of Practice that will give our customers a degree of confidence in what is still the uncertain and changing world of ebook publishing.

Publishing

The book is written and the time has come to find a reader. The road from writer to reader can be rocky but persevere and ensure you act as a professional. Submissions to magazines and Web sites follow the general principles outlined here, except it may be easier to contact the editors and to ask what material they require. The previous chapter dealt with ebooks, and there is no reason why an author cannot epublish their own work, and offer it for sale on their own Web site. There are several ecommerce facilities now available that allow money to be collected online, or a form can be placed on the Web site to be printed out by a prospective purchaser and sent to you, together with a cheque or International Money Order.

This chapter looks at the conventional publishing process, that of smearing ink on dead trees. It suggests that the author can undertake all these tasks for themselves. There are many thousands of books published by their authors. Some are very well-produced, and many have achieved notable sales. Normally a book's selling price can be broken down into several elements; costs of prepublication - editing, proofing, indexing, graphic design; of printing and production; author royalties; marketing and promotion; distribution costs; retailer discount - and, hopefully, profit.

Determining the selling price depends upon these elements. Don't believe that selling price is a vital marketing item. If a buyer wants a book it is unlikely that price will be a major issue. Ensure costs are covered.

ISBN

All books intended for commercial distribution, including ebooks, should have an ISBN. The International Standard Book Number (ISBN) identifies individual books. In the UK it is issued by Whitaker, Woolmead House West Bear Lane,

Farnham, Surrey GU9 7LG, website www.whitaker.co.uk. This 10 digit number identifies an individual book. Until recently blocks of ISBN numbers (10 was the minimum number) were issued to publishers free of charge. This is another service that has been converted to a cost centre and it now charges to issue an ISBN. However small-minded this may seem it is important to obtain an ISBN for all your publications as the title will then be entered into the national bibliography of books. An additional service is provided by Book Data and Whitaker who provide information about your books to interested parties.

That ISBN should be incorporated into a bar-code that also allows the retailer to add the price of the book. It may be wiser not to display the book's price on the cover as it can then be sold at a variety of prices; as promotions, special offers, even remaindered prices to clear away stocks.

Finding a Printer

The usual way to produce books is to find a printer who will then produce a stated number of copies of the book in paperback or hardback, with card covers or casebound. This is an enormous area, well beyond this book but there are some general statements that may be useful. Most books are produced in one print-run, and the publisher (that's you) must decide how many books should be printed. It is tempting to produce too many as the longer the print-run the lower the cost for each book. However if unsold books remain stacked up in the spare room the economy of the whole project will look very sad. The printer may resist but reprints to meet sales are the best way to proceed. Unit costs may be higher, but if you are selling every book at a profit, luxury will be yours.

Successful Negotiation

This is not to suggest that printers are difficult people. They are not, often they are very helpful but printing is complex. Negotiation means that both parties understand what is going to happen. To negotiate successfully requires that both parties are prepared to give and take, and that both parties have some understanding of the other person. Contract negotiations between author-publishers and printers often break down, so these hints may help both parties.

Communication is never easy. Communicating so that someone else will do what you want - can be very difficult, and often seem impossible. Several events can take place when someone hears your request;

The other person thinks, 'I am important and want to be respected'. Then they say to themselves, 'This person must consider MY needs' It is imperative that you listen at those formative stages. Next they are asking themselves, as you blurb away, ' How will the ideas of this person help ME?' Getting more rational, and beginning to accept your case, they then ask, ' What are the facts' Then move on to that crucial closing stage in the game, 'What shall I do?' Finally, you get, 'I approve', and they buy the deal, or 'I do not approve' and you have a hill to climb.

Preparation

Get to know the people involved - have a preliminary chat, perhaps about another subject. Find out something about them, in small deals this may not be over important but if a lasting relationship is to work it is good to know as much as you can about the other party - their personal life, the progress of their company.

Objectives

You want a book printed, at a reasonable price, to a set quality at an agreed time. Can you afford to lose out on some points, in order to gain advantage elsewhere. It will be a give-and-take process. The printer wants to achieve maximum throughput. Every moment the machinery stands idle is wasted time. Preparation time is wasted time, long runs are marvellous. Switch on the machine and walk away - that is the ideal state for any printer.

Structure

How much time will it take to do what needs to be done, and in what order will it be undertaken. Know how the print process works - what steps will be necessary - and how long each may take - it is useful to understand the problems the printer may face.

Conduct

The tactics of negotiation and the interpersonal behaviour that will take place during the discussions are major factors in the deal. Just as importantly the post- contract negotiations that may arise must always be borne in mind throughout the whole process. Never accept promises, only congratulate performance - by paying when the job is completed to your satisfaction - and not before.

Negotiating POWER

Promise a reward - you have something the other side wants (the printing job)

Threat of Punishment - if it is unacceptable you will withdraw - a valuable ploy in a recession, or you will spread the word amongst your friends and fellows.

Legitimacy - you know the facts, and your statements are true.

Other variables - knowing a personal friend, using a sympathy vote, insisting on a small detail - like delivery - as being of vital importance.

Confidence - you know what you want, and exude that knowledge.

Steps in Planning Negotiations

Aim High - it is easier to come down from the mountain. Separate out the elements that; You must have to make the deal worthwhile. Consider the ideal outcomes you wish to achieve and what parts of the overall contract you can allow to become loss leaders in order to obtain a good deal.

Deciding who will print your book may be one of the major financial decisions of your life. Perhaps not so important as buying a house but it may be equal to a new car, and will probably equal the cost of your annual holiday. Not to be undertaken lightly and preparation is important. It differs from the house, the car and the holiday in that it contains an infinite number of variations. The choices you make for each book are different - Ford will give you comparatively few options with that new car.

Once you understand your needs - look carefully at the printers requirements - what will they require from this deal? They will want to produce a good job, as quickly as possible, with minimum hassle - and make a profit. Remember profit is not a dirty word, without such incentives business becomes an unworkable sham. While offering no guarantees, we have prepared a basic set of questions to use when obtaining a quote from printers

The initial position you adopt will depend upon your own circumstances. Do you know enough about book production to be confident enough to understand the quotations you receive. Do you know enough about the printer, and their work to know they can produce the book you want, at the right quality, at a price and quantity you can afford?

The opening stance is meant to build bridges between yourself and the printer. There are many ways to establish that rapport. Face-to-face contact helps, you can open the discussion on a neutral subject, allay suspicion, assure that you want to gain agreement.

The basic Quotation has been received, now is the time to start negotiations.

Planning will have identified the concessions you are prepared to make. Concessions must be traded, very reluctantly, never given. Be seen to be driving a hard bargain (albeit sweetly), there will only be a limited number of concessions you can make - make each one count, draw as much out of each point as possible.

When making a Concession

Stress the cost to you. Exaggerate - but truthfully. Do not overstate, and provide evidence. Refer to major problems that you will suffer as a result of conceding. Imply that the concession is exceptional - I would never normally do that but ....

When the Other Party makes a concession

Do not overdo any expression of thanks, a curt acceptance is sufficient. Underplay the concession when it is made - say 'that is a small point, I suppose.' Divide the concession up into small units - say; 'that will save me 2p per book'. Treat them as expected outcomes, not concessions at all. Accept, but imply that it was not really necessary. Deny that the concession has any value.

Underplay any offer they make, inflate any concession you are forced into.

Tips to use when negotiating

Keep thinking all the time. Each word is important and keep looking for the unstated implications. Take time - there is no need to keep talking, silence can be very effective, especially when you have asked a difficult question. Wait and make them answer. Take notes, make any calculations necessary - involve the other party in that process, use it as a time to restate the case. Go through each step, and confirm the progress made. Make sure the printer is happy to proceed, and feels good about the negotiation. Build an agreement, do not have a fight. Try and remain neutral - imagine that this deal is not for you, often talking in the third person can help, with questions such as; 'Are you happy if people ask for a non-standard size of paper?'. Contain yourself until everything has been revealed before making that final offer on the deal. Time is rarely important - be flexible - and accommodating. Eventually, time is a negotiating variable - and rarely will you find it so important that a deadline cannot be extended. Remember nothing is ever 'fixed' everything can be changed, with negotiation.

Your personal behaviour is important - be aware of body language and of verbal signs. Phrases like 'I do not have the authority' must prompt (at some time) 'Well who does, let's talk to them'. 'Our price for that print run will be' ....'but for a larger quantity, on my stock paper, in September - not July when everyone is on holiday, in two colour, presented unbound etc. 'Those are the standard terms and conditions' but we could talk.

Make sure your motives are clear - hidden motives can prevent the printer from coming clean. Understand that you have had a clear answer to the question asked. If it is avoided, sidestepped or ignored - wonder and then ask, why. Keep calm, summarise the discussion at frequent intervals. This is not the place to consider the complications of negotiation in which you set out to deliberately unbalance the opposition, but that can be fun.

Printers must be seen as busy, intelligent and basically cooperative people. They want to do your job, at the best rate, in the easiest way - for them. Sub-contracting four colour printing because your chosen firm does not do four- colour work is doomed from the start for your printer has very little control, so make sure they do everything themselves - or have a very close relationship with someone who does.

Be very wary about those that demand payment before delivery. In fact, avoid them like the plague.

Print On Demand

Print on Demand (POD) offers the book a real future. Normally publishers use a standard printing process that relies upon printing a number of copies of a book at the same time. The more copies the cheaper the cost of each book and it is tempting to produce many thousands and then hope they can be sold. Deciding how many copies of a new book to publish can be a difficult decision, especially when the author is unknown. Naturally publishers tend to be conservative, most will only decide to publish when they can anticipate the chosen book will make a profit. There is a natural reluctance to risk good money on the unknown, and is a good reason why only 2,000 new novelists are published every year.

The United Kingdom publishes more new titles every year, currently around 100,000. The UK has fewer publishers than USA where about the same number of books are published each year. The US has the Publishers Marketing Association, www.pma-online.org with 3-4,000 members while the erstwhile Author Publisher Network that I helped to start years ago, and has now decayed, never reached far beyond 300 members. Small publishers have not flourished although the Independent Publishers Guild has an active membership that includes a number of eminent, if small, publishers.

The difference between the two countries is easy to spot. American publishers are active marketeers, ever-ready to promote their work whereas the average Brit seems to be too shy or they just expect success, not realising it needs application and hard work to achieve. That needs to change if author-publishing is to become acceptable.

Authors must continue to submit MSS to publishers but hopefully they will all begin to realise that publishers require good-quality work that will appeal to as many members of the public as possible. Authors must want to sell books. Do not send publishers unedited ill-considered life stories or eclectic collections of prose or poetry that will not sell as they will probably be rejected.

Going it Alone

Most publishers have huge piles of manuscripts waiting to be rejected. These 'slush piles' could be reduced considerably if authors appreciated more of the world of publishing. One simple way is to produce your own book and then try to sell it. It can be a salutary lesson but should be tackled by all budding authors. A simple way forward is to produce a simple booklet; nice colour photocopied card cover with stapled pages within. Sell it to friends, relatives and send it to potential publishers as part of your submission material. Remember that the first book is unlikely to be the best work you will ever produce, so be prepared to experiment with it, to throw caution to the wind and, above all, to stand up to be counted. This can be great fun; John Hegley, performance poet, started by making such small books of his poetry. One edition was covered with sandpaper, another wrapped in a carpet. Make it special; use it to test the world - to see if they are intelligent enough to read your work.

The next stage is to produce a book; real ink smeared on dead trees book that can be held, smelt, cherished and read. Until recently that facility was only available to authors prepared to pay extortionate sums to sharks, known collectively as vanity publishers. Now, there is an alternative - Print On Demand. At author.co.uk we are linked to both book distributors and short-run printing specialists. Together we offer a variety of options that allow us to prepare a book for publication. It is then stored on a computer waiting until someone orders a copy of the book.

At author.co.uk we act the role of publisher in that we decide which books will enter the system. Our primary concern is quality. It is vital, absolutely vital, to the whole process of shortening the space between writer and reader that the book involved in that transfer from one brain to another can demonstrate it has been properly produced. At author.co.uk we ensure all the pre-publications processes are undertaken to ensure the final product reads well and looks good. It is then sent to the printer who use the latest Xerox technology to produce the book; one copy at a time that is then sent to the distributors, both in UK and North America.

The POD process is extremely useful for new work or for books that will not sell in large numbers. At author.co.uk we offer three basic services;

Torremolinos Approach

The first is for authors who do not expect their book to be a commercial success. It is the Torremolinos Approach; an alternative to a holiday abroad that fulfils an ambition and produces a worthy product that the author will be proud to sell or give to friends and family.

That book can be a personal biography, a family history, an academic paper, a non-fiction manual, a book of school lesson plans, a collection of poetry or a novel. Anything can be considered as material for a book provided it meets basic quality standards. It may be that a small number of copies are required as review copies, to be produced well before the actual publication date of the title or to be sent to a publisher as an example of your work. There are any number of reasons why authors may need our Starting Service and we hope to meet most requests. The author undertakes to purchase an initial quantity of books at an agreed discount, usually 35% of the selling price. A book that will sell for £10 will be sold to the author at £6.50, so enabling the author to sell the book to bookshops. If author.co.uk sells additional copies, in whatever manner, the author will receive a royalty on all those sales.

Author Publishing Ltd

The second service is for books that are intended to enter the commercial market. In this case Author Publishing Ltd (the company that owns author.co.uk) will normally act as publisher, with each author published under a separate imprint. We undertake all the costs of production, paying the author an agreed royalty (never less than 10%). We will promote and market the book, which will form part of the growing list of Author Publishing titles. We impose demands upon authors just as any other publisher but will usually be prepared to take greater risks.

Reprint Service

Third service: a reprint service where we scan in the contents of an existing book to reproduce a new master digital file. Using scanning equipment and sophisticated text and image handling software we can bring an old book back to life - for the copyright holder. The copy required for this process will be destroyed in the process but even so this allows out-of-print books to be made available once again, at costs that fall well below those of full origination. Once the copy has been digitised it can be considered for either of the above services.

For all services the published book is made available as a POD book, with an ISBN and inclusion in the National Bibliography and the stocklists of major distributors. It will also have its own page at the author.co.uk Web site and be part of all the marketing and promotional activities of Author Publishing Ltd. If required an Ebook version is produced or a sample chapter is made for display at author.co.uk and its affiliate sites.

We are also willing to help author-publishers or small publishing companies by providing a POD and Ebook publishing and distribution service tailored to meet demands.

Dreams not always Perfect

Print On Demand is an answer to many dreams but it is just another tool in the authors' armoury and on its own is not a complete answer. First of all the author must write a book that wants to be read. That book must be properly edited and proofread and be made ready for publication so that the final book is easy to the eye and attractive to read. In most cases professional support will be required to get a book ready for publication. Too many writers believe they can edit and judge the merits of their own work. That is a ridiculous myth. Pre-publication services of editing, proofreading, indexing and graphic design are all necessary and cannot be avoided.

Print on Demand offers authors and readers the chance to experiment with new ideas, and it is these that will move us all forward. There will be serious mistakes made but who needs perfection?

Selling Books

Writers need to know something about the commercial markets for their books. It is important to keep abreast of developments even if that only means an occasional stroll through a local bookstore and a glance at the best-sellers on display.

Bookshops

Bookshops are under threat. Increasingly books are sold via the Internet; note that you can buy any one of 285,000 titles online at author.co.uk, at a discount. Even so online bookstores are not making a profit and like so many so-called dot.com companies they are waking up to the realities of direct marketing, requiring advertising on TV, magazines and newspapers, and distribution, which is a highly skilled business in itself. Our author.co.uk bookstore obtains books from Gardners, the largest book distributor in the UK.

Online

Many online stores have an enormous list of titles, most of which are not held in their own warehouses but are obtained as required from book wholesalers. Once digital television starts to gain wider acceptance book sales are expected to soar, as TV takes the Net into 22 million more UK households.

Threats

Online stores challenge the town bookshops that also face other dangers, often of their own making. The large retailer W H Smith only stocks a few hundred titles, and these are carefully chosen and maintained. Shelves in stores are constantly monitored; with the management aware of how much money a particular shelf display should be gathering in every week. If a book fails to reach the expected income it is removed. A book-pulping machine sits in the main warehouse ever ready to accept economic failures. This lack of shelf storage space is revealed by the short-term but intensive exposure that is given to new books. Listen to the radio, watch TV, notice the front windows of bookshops to see the face of the same author appearing time and time again for a few weeks. A few short days later it is removed and replaced by the next in line. Ask for a first-time novelist's book in the shops a few months later and it may not be available.

Recently Waterstones, the UK's largest retailer of books seems to have been taken over by people with little understanding of books. It is alleged that one memo sent out by the company instructed that managers must only interview those publishers' representatives whose books sold well. Such an approach does nothing to encourage new talent; writers or publishers. The range of choice found on shelves is declining. Whether that will encourage readers to read more book reviews or to search for information about the books they could read is difficult to quantify. Some publishers are beginning to recognise that readers' groups can exert a powerful influence.

Libraries

It is a tragedy that spending on libraries has dropped by 12 per cent across Britain over the last ten years, and by 45 per cent in London, according to a recent report by the National Book Committee. Recognising that dreadful situation is not enough; we need to divert funds back into this essential national resource. Libraries are trying to keep at the centre of information provision; often providing Internet access, DVD's, audio-books and much more but they suffer from such woefully inadequate funding. As writers it is important that we all keep up a barrage of complaints against the petty-minded accountants who are inhibiting our national creativity for short-term gains.

Publishers today

Many major publishers are cutting down on the number of titles they carry. Traditionally a publisher has relied upon the income flowing from a back-list of titles they produced in earlier years each of which continues to attract a regular stream of orders. Cutting back on stock reduces the costs of warehousing, insurance and distribution but also reduces potential income.

Bookselling Future

Book sales are falling, not by huge percentages but with growing significance. It reinforces the need to look for solutions. Those of the accountant will never be satisfactory. Restoration of spending by libraries and in education would help. Distribution systems could be improved, and a return to some form of Net Book Agreement may be necessary. The NBA imposed a regulatory control upon the selling price of a book. Its removal has allowed some large stores and even supermarkets to cream off the large sales of best-selling books by offering these for sale at discounts that the small bookshops cannot counter. Many small bookshops have already disappeared and more will follow yet it is significant to note that second-hand bookshops often remain.

Authors selling books

Where shall we turn to sell books? For the author there is merit in looking at quality rather than quantity. The publisher is concerned with volume, the need to sell more and more, to keep the treadmill moving forward. The author can take another perspective. They have taken a year or more to produce the book, and often find it galling to see it removed from the system within days of publication. One answer is to keep the pot boiling, get out amongst the teeming populace to maintain awareness of your book. All publishers have a publicity department, and most do a fine job, but they can be helped enormously by an author who is willing to get involved. Well before the book is published the author needs to start a personal publicity campaign. This must start with a list of all potential markets - decide who will buy this book. Who are they? What magazines will they read, which associations do they belong to, where are they likely to live? Build a picture of the person who will soon be holding your book in their hands.

Target Audiences

Once the potential customers have been identified they must be targeted. Write a number of articles that cover the subject area of your book and send these off to the selected magazines. These must be sent in good time, months before the publication date and make sure that each article contains a timely reference to your book, giving the date of publication, name of publisher and ISBN and, most importantly, the title and your name.

Contacts

Contact all the associations on your list and offer to send an article for their newsletter and to give talks to their local groups. This is a time consuming business but authors must take the term view if you are not to be a 'one-book wonder'. Writing is to become your life, your world, and it is imperative that people know your name. There is an old marketing adage that says once people have heard a name seven times that name will gain credibility, just because it has entered brains again and again. It's the principle that purveyors of fizzy sugary drinks use to great effect. Authors should follow their example; write to local newspapers, invite yourself onto local radio, do not miss an opportunity at self-aggrandisement.

Advance Information

The publisher should have sent out any number of Advance Information Sheets (AIS) well before publication. These go to booksellers, libraries and reviewers giving basic information on one side of an A4 sheet; title, author, technical details, who will buy the book and a short blurb together with contact details. They may also issue a press release; written in a magazine article style that journalists can use to easily produce their own piece. Work closely with your publicist to discover where you can attend book signings, or subject yourself to a detailed interview with a journalist. Be available. There is a myth that writers tend to be shy retiring creatures shunning publicity. Most successful authors are not like that, indeed they will fall over themselves to help others spread the word - about them and their books.

Internet Presence

Every author must have a Web site. Not any old freebie that gives an obscure URL (Unique Reference Locator - Web site eddress). It is important to obtain a domain name, or to ensure your site will remain a permanent fixture (as far as that is possible with the Net). The site can be used as a catalogue that is permanently available to which anyone can be referred for information.

One Option

An old friend of mine, Michael Birch, wrote and published a dozen books. Years ago he bought a duplex printer, to print both sides of the paper at once, and a small book-binding machine. He wrote, printed, produced and published all his books from one small room in his home. At any time he tried to maintain a stock of thirty books of each title on the shelves, knowing that his steady sales would only rarely take more of his stock. One day of his week was spent as a book producer, another as a publisher, most of the rest as a writer.

He knew his market and kept up a constant barrage of material to interest potential buyers. Importantly he calculated that he made as much profit from one book handed over to the reader in exchange for cash as he did when sending fifty-six books to a major retailer through a distributor. In the first case he had paid for a full colour card cover, for the paper and ink and his own time, the rest was profit. In the latter case the profit had to be extracted from the forty per-cent left after posting the books to a distributor (in the hope that they would not all be returned later).

Michael Birch's case is stated only to make authors realise that there may be other ways to reach readers than relying upon conventional publishers. The task of going it alone is daunting, but possible. Avoid vanity publishers, they will bring nothing but grief, but there are a small number of book production specialists who can take the author through the process of publishing their own work.

The End of the Beginning

This book has quickly scraped over the surface of the world of the writer. It is not meant to do much more than act upon the taste-buds of your imagination. We will be at author.co.uk to give you advice and support if required.

Now it is your turn. Start writing or looking over that manuscript with fresh eyes and start finding readers.

You owe it to yourself.

Index

A

A4 15
academic 21
accessible writing 171
accident 55
actors 27
actress 27
Adobe Acrobat 17, 27
Adobe Ebook Reader 265
adult education centre 217
Advance Information Sheets 289
agents 49
AIS 289
Albert Ellis 57
Amolibros 20
Amstrad 11
anagram 17
anti-war 214
AOL 238
Apple 11
argument 201
Arthur Conan Doyle 83
article writing 43
Arts Council 217
ASCII 16
aspirations 6
Association of Authors' Agents, The 259
atmosphere 79
attraction 98
audience 5, 251
audio 8
audio journal 35
author interviews 19
Author Publishing Ltd 282
author.co.uk 4, 5, 27
autobiography 56
automatic writing 39

B

back-up 11
backache 5
behaviour 58
belief 175
Bernie Ross 76
Bertolt Brecht 101
Bertrand Russell 173
bible 87
Bill Thompson 174
biography 5, 27, 56, 57, 58
Blake Friedmann 49
Blamires 15
blind writing 152
blindfold 52
body language 97
Book Data 272
book printing 273
bookshop 7
bookshops 285
brainstorming 33
Brian Baker 137
British Council 24
Buckingham Palace 81
building 80
bursaries 24
business 261

C

California 20
Canon John Collins 173
Carl Rogers 66
Carole Blake 23, 261
CD-I 243
CD-ROM 11, 243
chain letters 236
character 56, 57, 127
character sketches 100
characters 25
civil servant 26
Clare Short MP 175
cliché 87
clichés 48
comedy 158, 171
comics 159
competition 22
complexity 107
computer 16
computers 11
concept 7
confidentiality 45
contacts 239
content providers 223
contracts 246
conversation 88
copy editing 249
copyright 241, 248
Copyright Act 247
CPM 11
creative 5, 105

creative energy 178
creative process 143
creative writers 44
creative writing courses 21
creativity 5
crime 22, 158
Crime Writers Association 23
critique services 65
cross-gender 85
Curtis Brown 20
Cyril Connolly 81
Cytale 265

D

Data Protection Act 228
Dave Feakes 219
David Lodge 21
David Smail 204
debate 201
Deborah Tannen 85
Denmark 25
description 33, 154
design 227
detail 65, 103
detective
    thrillers
        spy 162
detritus 35
dialogue 35, 91, 251
diaries 31
dictaphone 15
dictionary 13, 15
Dictionary of Clichés 87
different 52
digital material 13
digital works
    electronic works 243
directories 225
discussion 220
disguise 39
distance 40
ditties 152
documentaries 36
domain name 227, 231
Don Van Vliet 70
DOS 11
Douglas Adams 55
drama 66
dreams 6
ducks 68
Durlabh Singh 26
DVD 243

E

ebook publishing 265
ebook readers 264
ebooks
    Electronic publishing 8
eddress 228
Edinburgh 22
editing 249
editor 48
electronic publishing
    ebooks 263
elegant writing 77
Ellie McLoughlin 187
email 224, 234
Emlyn Rees 20
emotions 181
empathise 173
encouragement 4
ending 130
English 14
Enid Blyton 57
envelopes 15
Epictetus 42
Eric Partridge 78
erotica 162
escape 25
European Union 238
evening class 109
exercises 67
experience 58, 137
experiences 40
experimental writing 151
experts 22
explore 132
extracts 247

F

facial expressions 34
Fact 5
fact 5
fantasy 66, 161
features editor 45
feelings 182
feely games 53
Felixstowe 219
fellowships 24
fiction 5, 7, 250
filing cabinet 16
film 112, 243
Fingerlickin 83
finishing
    writing the end 130

firewalls 239
flash fiction 160
floppy disks 12
Florence Nightingale 58
folders 16
Franklin eBookman 265
Freddy Macha 28
freedom 51, 185
freewriting 32, 36
friends 40
frolics 67
frustration 5
fun 68

G

Gardners Books 255
gender 84
genre 23, 157
Geoff Pridmore 24
George Bernard Shaw 101
George Szirtes 24
ghosts 162
Glassbook 265
goals 5
Gold Dagger 23
google 225
gossip 55
graffiti 152
grammar 13, 39, 99
grants 24
graphic novels 159
Greek Legends 87
grouching therapy 43

H

hackers
    Firewalls 239
hand 53
hang-ups 53
hard disks 12
Harry Blamires 78
Harry Potter 77
Henry VIII 59
Hiebook 265
Hilary Johnson 65
historical 161
Hodder & Stoughton 25
honesty 4
horror 159, 211
HTML 265
Hungary 24
Hypertext Mark-Up
Language 265

I

Ian McEwan 149
Ian Rankin 22
icons 59
identity 91
imagination 7, 135
immortality 6
impressions 99
independent press
    small press magazines 161
Independent Publishers
Guild 279
indexing 253
inferiority complex 46
ink-jet 13
Instant Whip 74
intensive writing 35
interactive dialogue 92
International Standard Book
Number 271
Internet 13, 26, 223, 231
Internet Service Provider 238
interviews 15
Introduction 1
introduction 1
ISBN 271
ISP
    Internet Service Provider 238

J

Jacquie Bennett 65
Jancis Robinson 28
Jane Tatam 20
Jilly Cooper 56
John Dawes 27
John Gray 85
John Hegley 26
John Spurling 27
John Steinbeck 172
Josie Lloyd 20
journal 31
journalist 24
Joy Larkcom 21
Julian Stockwin 23, 261
junk mail 235

K

Kiliminjaro 28
kill fee 45

Koran 87

L

laser printer 13
Lawrence Durrell 148
Lego 73
length 7
letter size 15
liberation 51
libraries 286
library 7, 217
life 55
life experiences 64
life history 59
Linux 11
list
    index
        Table of Contents 14
listen 89
lists 33
literary agents
20, 23, 49, 259
literary clout 171
Literary Consultancy, The 65
literary genre 157
Literature Officer 217
local history 50
locations 25
loneliness 5

M

Macromedia 17
magazine 50
magazine fiction 160
magic carpet 110
magic realism 161
magnetism 12, 13
mailing lists 237
Malcolm Bradbury 21
manipulation 105
manuscript 8
Margot Strickland 27
Maura 27
maze 155
meditative writing 34
mental relaxation 68
mental stimulation 51
metaphor 40
metaphors 106, 153
Michael Birch 289
microphone 35
Microsoft 16

mind-reading 62
mirror dialogue 154
mission statement 6
mobile phone 52
mood 79
movies
    film 159
MS 8
MS Reader 265
MS Word 16
MSS 8, 49
multi-media 8, 243
music 79
myths 242

N

Nadine Gordimer 147
NANAE 238
narrative 61, 129
National Association of Writers in Education 28
National Consumers League 236
National Office of Digital Archiving (NODA) 12
National Preservation Office 11
nature 52
naval history 23
negatives 153
negotiation 272
newsgroups
    Mailing Lists 237
newspaper 88
Nobel Peace Prize 214
Nobel Prize 148
non-fiction 5, 22, 157
Norfolk 24
novel 161
novels 56
nursery rhyme 84, 101, 155

O

objectives 3
obscure 153
observation 103
observations 65
observe 80
on-line 243

P

P.G. Wodehouse 147
Pablo Picasso 143
pain 145

painter 26
painting 103
Palm 265
paper 15
paper clips 16
parable 87
parody 171
partnership 20
Partridge 15
paternity 244
pdf files
    Adobe Acrobat
        Acrobat 263
peace 214
Pearsall Smith 81
pen
pencil
    hand 53
pen name 45
pencil 13
Penelope Lively 24
penury 5
permissions 247
perspective 7
Philip Larkin 147
Phillip II of Spain 59
philosophy 171
play 27, 68
plays 91
playwright 27
plays
    stage plays 159
plot 127
plots 251
POD
    Print on Demand 279
poet 22
    performance poet 26
poetry 158
Polemia 210
politicians 25
politics 51
portraits 34
pose 151
potager 21
power games 96
predicaments 127
preservation 11
press release 222
pretend 80
printer 272
printing 13
Private Eye 146

private view 144
prizes 23, 24
problem pages 60
professional 25, 49
professional approach 23
professionals 29
promotional catalogue 232
prompts 33
proofreading 249
psychologists 66
publisher 8, 246, 255
Publishers Association 247
publishing 271

Q

quality 81
Queen Mary 59
quilt 153

R

radio diaries 35
ragtime 154
random word generators 17
Raymond Chandler 19
read 215
reader 5
readability factor 14
reading 126
recognition 48
reference books 15
reflective writing 34
rejection 47
relatives 40
remaindered 22
research 45
rights 244
Rocket ebook 265
role-play 68
romance 161
romantic erotica 162
rostrum 148
Rowling, Joanne 77
RTF (Rich Text Format) 16
rumour 55

S

sad endings 132
SAE 49
sample chapters
 records 257
Sandi Toksvig 25
scandal 55

scanner 17
scarecrow 233
science fiction 161
scissors 16
screen play 47
search engines 225
self-publishing 280
selling 285
sensations 25
serial rights 244
Shakespeare 84
Sheila Dainow 204
short stories 160
short story 8
short-run printing 8
show 78
Sigmund Freud 66
signs 97
similes 107
sitcoms 159
site assessment 227
slipstream 161
small press magazines 161
Society of Editors and
 Proofreaders 252
Society of Authors 26
Society of Authors, The
 242, 247, 259
Society of Indexers 254
software 11, 16
SPAM 235
Spamcop.net 238
specialist writer 43
spell check 13
spelling 39
spiritual experience 143
Stanley Spencer 57
stapler 16
start 128
starting to write 3
stories 56
structure 135
Strunk 15
style 77
sub-editor 46
submission 256
subsidiary rights 245
subsidy publishers 259
Suffolk County library 216
surrealist 151
Susan Perry 19
swimming pools 27
symbolism 40, 171

symptoms 97
synopsis 84, 257

T

tabloid press 25
taboo 152
tape drives 12
tape record 53
tape recorder 15, 35
tell 78
tenses 250
Terminated 187
theatre 27
therapy 39
thesaurus 13, 15
third party 34
third person 39
Thomas Mann 145
thought 55
Tom Sharpe 15
trade publishers 8
tragedy 84
travel 52
treasure 88
triggers 87
truth 5
Tutankhamen 81
TV
 television 159
typewriter 13
typist 13

U

Universal Copyright
 Convention 241
University of East Anglia 21
Unix 11
unsolicited copy 48
Usage & Abusage 78

V

Vaclev Havel 101
vanity 259
vanity publisher 268
vanity publishers 220
vegetable 21
video 243
viewpoint 61
viewpoints 250
vignette 82
vignettes 71
virus 236
visual images 89

visualise 103
vivid prose 126
voice 51, 61, 155
voices 83
voluntary 50

W

Wang 11
wannabees 19
war 161
warnings 224
water
   paint 69
Waterstones 286
web
   WWW
      world wide web 224
Web design 17
web site 232
web sites 223, 243
Whitaker 271
White House, The 81
whodunnit
   mystery 162
why write 4
wider world 215
Winchester Writers' Weekend 24
Windows 11
wine 28
women's magazine 160
word-processing 12
World Atlas of Wine 28
writers' circles 216
Writing Life 54

Y

yourself 31
Yvonne Fern 57

Z

zip drives 12